"In this companion set of Compassion Focused Group Therapy guides for group facilitators and for group participants, the authors have created a remarkably accessible resource that promotes deeply humane, high quality clinical care. The manuals are written with the wisdom of experienced group therapists utilizing a structured, well- defined and well-researched model of compassion focused care. These therapy guides address the implementation gap that so often exists between theory and clinical practice in ways that are particularly relevant for today's group therapists and their clients."

—**Molyn Leszcz, MD, FRCPC, CGP, DFAGPA,**
professor of Psychiatry, University of Toronto; president,
the American Group Psychotherapy Association

"This manual and workbook is a tour de force! Compassion focused therapy (CFT) is a powerful, multi-dimensional, scientifically-based approach to managing difficult emotions. The authors have brilliantly condensed CFT into twelve, easily digestible modules. This could be the most valuable course a student takes in college—learning to regulate emotions by cultivating a compassionate mind. Highly recommended for young and old!"

—**Christopher Germer, PhD,**
lecturer (part-time), Harvard Medical School; co-author,
Teaching the Mindful Self-Compassion Program

"Compassion Focused Therapy embodies the major tenets of the APA-accredited group psychology and group psychotherapy specialty. It gives essential instruction for leaders and members, presenting the ideas in well written text with great graphics. This program takes the practitioner through the steps and issues central to initiating, managing, and practicing group therapy in college counseling settings in a manner that lines up nicely with the guidelines of the group specialty."

—**Joshua M. Gross, PhD, ABPP,**
director of Group Programs; licensed psychologist

"Highly recommended are the manual and workbook for *Compassion Focused Group Therapy for University Counseling Centers.* These present a sequence of group sessions that clinicians will find as excellent guidance for group facilitation and members will help structure their own personal development. The authors are to be commended for developing these evidence-based publications that are well researched, written and are shown to benefit group to grow, develop and heal."

— **Nina W. Brown, EdD,**
professor and eminent scholar, Old Dominion University;
distinguished fellow, American Group Psychotherapy Association;
fellow American Psychological Association

"The last 20 years has seen an explosion of research into the physiological and psychological effects of compassion training, and how to make compassion central to psychotherapeutic endeavours. In this beautifully written and easily accessible work internationally renowned group researcher and psychotherapist Gary Burlingame and his team outline a group modular approach for young people attending University with mental health difficulties. With their already excellent research findings and programme, all group therapist will gain enormously from the wisdoms, clarity and guidance offered here."

— **Professor Paul Gilbert,**
OBE, author of The Compassionate Mind (2009);
Compassion Focused Therapy *(2010); president*
of the Compassionate Mind Foundation

"This manual skillfully blends the content and process driven elements of short term CFT groups, whilst offering creativity and concrete guidance. This is an absolute gift to our CFT community and will be essential reading for all those Compassion Focused Therapists who are motivated to explore the affiliative possibilities of group based CFT. This manual also reflects the wealth of experience and knowledge in groupwork practice brought by the authors."

— **Kate Lucre, PhD,**
psychotherapist, Birmingham and Solihull Mental Trust

"Compassion Focused Therapy (CFT) is a powerful approach to mental health. It puts compassion as the central therapeutic target, with research showing it helps improve neurophysiology, mental health, interpersonal relations and pro-social behaviour with a diverse range of difficulties. This new manual is an excellent guide to implementing group CFT. The authors have provided exceptional guidance, clear dialogue examples, insightful graphics and metaphors that bring key CFT concepts to life. This manual will transform the way you deliver CFT."

— **James N. Kirby, PhD,**
senior lecturer and clinical psychologist

Compassion Focused Therapy Participant Workbook

Compassion Focused Therapy Participant Workbook is a companion book to *Compassion Focused Group Therapy for University Counseling Centers*, a one-of-a-kind 12-session manual for conducting compassion focused group therapy on college campuses.

Compassion-based interventions have been shown to decrease symptoms of depression, anxiety, and psychological distress in students. This book's 12 sessions incorporate several aspects of compassionate living including defining and understanding compassion, mindfulness, shame, assertiveness, and forgiveness to help participants act in more compassionate ways with themselves and others, lower feelings of shame and self-criticism, and engage in self-reassuring behaviors. The workbook provides clients with summaries of each session, handouts, and key exercises and, along with the manual, can be followed session-by-session or adapted according to the needs of the group.

This workbook is designed to be used by clinicians and participants in a clinician-led group utilizing *Compassion Focused Group Therapy for University Counseling Centers*.

Rachel Arnold is a graduate student at Brigham Young University studying clinical psychology. She is involved in clinical work and group therapy research.

Cameron T. Alldredge is completing his doctoral internship in a university counseling center. As an emerging psychologist, he is passionate about teaching, research, and clinical practice.

Kara Cattani is a clinical professor and director of Student Development Services at Brigham Young University. She divides her time between administrative work, clinical practice, training of graduate students, consulting, and clinical research.

Derek Griner is a practicing board-certified counseling psychologist with significant CFT experience. His research focuses on diversity issues for which he received APA's Division 17 award for excellence in scholarship.

David M. Erekson is a board-certified psychologist and an associate clinical professor at Brigham Young University. A dedicated scientist-practitioner, he has an active clinical practice and a psychotherapy research lab.

Gary M. Burlingame has contributed over 75 books, manuals and chapters and 150 articles on effective small group treatments and is president-elect of the American Group Psychotherapy Association.

Mark E. Beecher is a board-certified counseling psychologist who has practiced in a college counseling center for over 20 years. His practice and research interests include individual/group psychotherapy, CFT, and multicultural competence.

Compassion Focused Therapy Participant Workbook

**Rachel Arnold, Cameron T. Alldredge,
Kara Cattani, Derek Griner, David M. Erekson,
Gary M. Burlingame, Mark E. Beecher**

Routledge
Taylor & Francis Group

NEW YORK AND LONDON

First published 2022
by Routledge
605 Third Avenue, New York, NY 10158

and by Routledge
2 Park Square, Milton Park, Abingdon, Oxon, OX14 4RN

Routledge is an imprint of the Taylor & Francis Group, an informa business

Library of Congress Cataloging-in-Publication Data
A catalog record for this title has been requested

ISBN: 978-1-032-06484-0 (hbk)
ISBN: 978-1-032-06482-6 (pbk)
ISBN: 978-1-003-20249-3 (ebk)

DOI: 10.4324/9781003202493

Typeset in Times NR MT Pro
by KnowledgeWorks Global Ltd.

Contents

Handouts

How to Use This Workbook

We are providing this workbook material as a supplement to your group experience. The materials are meant to provide an overview of each module. Each module is separate and, depending on your group leader, may take up to three sessions of group work. Each module begins with a few pages that describe some of the core information that your leader will discuss with the group. Each module also has a copy of handouts that will be used or referred to by the leader. Some of these handouts are simply informational, while others help you and your leader work through exercises in the group. Each session will include soothing rhythm breathing and behavioral practice. We are happy to have you in this group with us, and hope that this workbook will be helpful to you as we experience this compassion focused therapy group together.

what is compassion?

tricky brain

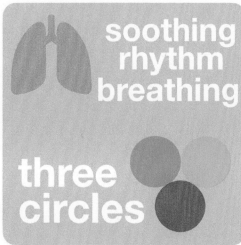

soothing rhythm breathing

three circles

focused attention

mindfulness

feeling safe

other selves

compassionate-self

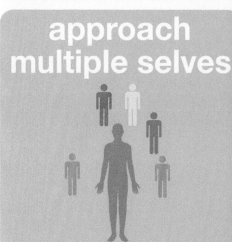

approach multiple selves

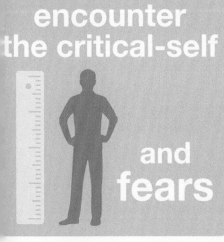

encounter the critical-self

and fears

healing from shame

it's not your fault

compassionate letter writing

compassionate assertiveness

compassion for others

forgiveness

moving forward

with a compassionate mind

Introduction & Welcome

Welcome to this compassion focused therapy group program. As a starting point, let's explore what we mean by compassion. Sometimes people think compassion is a sort of weakness or a bit soft or floppy. In reality we're going to see that compassion is about building courage and understanding in order to be able to work with things that have caused us pain and suffering. It certainly isn't soft or fluffy. We suspect in your heart you know this. Suppose you had a child who was in distress or a good friend who was very frightened of an upcoming medical appointment. How would you want to be with them? Think about that for a moment—think about what it is you would be trying to do, maybe to help calm them or maybe to help give them courage to face what they need to face. If you see compassion from this point of view, you will get a good understanding of what it is about. Compassion is also about treating ourselves with respect, support, and helpfulness rather than criticism, anger, and resentment. As we will learn during this group, relating to ourselves through criticism and anger can actually make us feel much, much worse.

The group you are about to undertake brings together an understanding of what is helpful to people; an understanding collected for over thousands of years, supported by the latest research on how our bodies and brains work when they experience compassion. In some ways, learning to stimulate compassion is like learning to drive a car. At first it can seem awkward and even frightening, but as we do it more, it gets easier and then we can even come to enjoy it. All new things in life often take a little time to settle in.

Compassion is a skill set, or ability, that we can build and strengthen. It is like training to run a marathon—we wouldn't start training by running a marathon straight away. We would take small steps and gradually build up our fitness, and eventually be able to complete the marathon. Importantly, as we work through this program, we are taking small steps to build this compassion muscle.

Starting any group can bring thoughts of uncertainty. For example, if we go to have surgery, we can be anxious and uncertain about what's going to happen. Will it work? When we start group therapy, we can have a whole range of similar thoughts that can keep us from attending the group! So, it's a courageous act that you are already a part of this group.

It can feel a little uncomfortable or unfamiliar sharing memories and challenges in a new group. Some of us would have had lives where we haven't really had an opportunity to explore our emotions because there have not been many (or any) people around us who would listen or, if they did listen, they criticized us. So, we will spend some time sharing and exploring in our group.

One thing that may help you connect and have a sense of being like others is to think about the fact that we are all made basically the same way—we grow to similar heights, have roughly the same life span, have amazing brains with a capacity for emotion built right in, and are created by nature and our genes. These genes have all been built for you *not by you*. The things in your brain that allow you to feel joy, anxiety, anger, sadness, hope, despair, and more are also, again, built *for* you but not by you. Nature has built a brain for you that makes it possible for you feel those feelings.

The problem is that sometimes our emotions can get a little too intense and can be difficult to understand, and at times can literally take us over. Getting anxious if you see smoke coming under the door or if you hear the roar of a lion close by is useful. It's less useful when we can't stop feeling anxious—we ruminate and worry, even if we know that anxiety in the current moment is not useful and we'd rather not have those feelings. So, learning how to understand and work with our emotions can be really helpful to us, particularly when we take a compassionate orientation to them and realize that we experience the emotions we do because that's how nature has built them into us. It's not our fault.

Not only are our emotions built into us by nature, but our emotions are also organized by past life experiences. Had we been born into different circumstances, we could be entirely different. This may be odd and difficult to think about; we have such a strong sense of who we are, when in reality we have been strongly influenced

DOI: 10.4324/9781003202493-1

by past situations. These past experiences have helped us build our strong sense of who we are by shaping different emotions and motives. For example, maybe if we did not feel loved as children, we can feel sad when we think how we might have turned out if we had been loved. Perhaps we have developed many harmful behavioral patterns based on past situations and relationships. It takes courage and compassion to acknowledge and see clearly how our lives are working currently. Rather than blame ourselves, we want to commit ourselves to try to create the versions of us that will be helpful. Fortunately, we can learn to understand and respond to difficult emotions effectively by developing mindfulness and compassion, and by making choices about what we want to do and how we want to behave in the world. In other words, we can learn to drive our minds and help guide it in the direction that we want to go.

This workbook has been developed to be used alongside your group sessions with your therapist. It is divided into 12 modules, and there are a series of exercises for you to have a go at, as well as information you can read. We hope this will help you to apply the ideas from the group sessions to your everyday life. Your group therapist will help you work through the program, and will answer any questions you might have.

Module 1: Introduction, Compassion, & Tricky Brain

Aims

- Establish group rules, norms, and safety.
- Define what compassion is and is not.
- Discuss the flows of compassion.
- Talk about our tricky brains and evolutionary theory.
- Discuss ways our minds get into unhelpful loops that we have the power to change.
- Explore compassionate wisdom.
- Wrap up with a compassionate cultivation meditation.

DOI: 10.4324/9781003202493-2

what is compassion?

tricky brain

Introduction

Compassion focused therapy (CFT) is an approach that focuses on the interplay between biology, psychology, and your social environment. Our goal is to increase wisdom and understanding of how our hardware (brain) and software (past experiences) affect our daily lived experience. In each session, we will spend time learning skills that provide alternative ways to handle life.

In the first module we talk a bit about *what compassion is* and *what compassion is not*.

Compassion **is**:

- **"Sensitivity to suffering and distress in self and others with a commitment to try to alleviate and prevent it." One insightful group member in another group summarized all this as "empathy in action."**

Compassion **is not**:

- just being kind,
- feeling sorry for others,
- being submissive…in fact, compassion can be quite assertive.

Sometimes, in order to better understand what compassion is, it can be useful to think about very compassionate people you know. What makes them compassionate? What do they do and say? How do these people behave?

We all need compassion because we all just find ourselves here with a **tricky brain** having to cope with the ups and downs of life. Essentially, our brain was built **for us, not by us**. We have **genes** we did not choose and do not get to control. We are **socially constructed**, or shaped, by our experiences. While it's **not our fault** that our minds are like they are, **it is our responsibility** to learn how to work with our minds. For example, imagine you had been kidnapped as a three-day-old baby and grew up in a very different environment. You would obviously be a very different version of yourself.

Despite the fact that we are influenced by things we didn't choose, we have the ability to be aware of ourselves and to monitor our minds. We can ruminate about the past and the future. This tricky brain leads us to develop feedback loops, thoughts about a threat that lead to unpleasant emotions, that lead to some type of action, that lead to more thoughts, and round it goes. These feedback loops often times are not very helpful. This ability to ruminate is not our fault, but it is our responsibility.

For example, imagine a zebra running away from a lion. Once they get away and can no longer see, hear, or smell the lion, there is nothing to keep them anxious, and in fact they settle down quite quickly. While a human will also be quite relieved to escape a lion, we tend to have thoughts such as: "Can you imagine if I'd been caught and what would it be like to be eaten by a lion?!" Our minds can suppose and create many frightening possibilities. Zebras don't do anything like this!

One of the aims of CFT is to help us recognize that there are several different versions of ourselves and start looking at the ways we can get stuck in patterns of thinking and feeling that are unhelpful. We are working toward choosing the version of ourselves we want to become; specifically, we hope to develop the compassionate version of ourselves.

One of the first steps we can take is acknowledging our **compassionate wisdom.** Our compassionate wisdom consists of recognizing that we are all just here with a very tricky brain and life experiences that we didn't choose. This is part of what it means to be human. This compassionate wisdom reminds us that we are not alone—everyone has a tricky brain, and this helps us experience a sense of common or shared humanity with those around us. It helps us see the wisdom in the phrase, "It's not my fault, but it is my responsibility."

Ground Rules for Working Together

Respecting & supporting each other

- We agree to respect each other and the courage of coming here.
- We try to support each other as best as we can.

Sharing experiences

- No pressure to talk if one doesn't wish to, yet we all will try to encourage each other with kindness to face things that we might find difficult.
- If someone is feeling distressed about a topic, it is okay for us to pause and focus on that before moving on.

Keeping confidentiality

- All personal experiences we discuss are confidential.
- We agree to keep things only in the group so members can feel safe.

Being open minded

- We all come from different places and have different experiences. So, we try not to think in terms of right or wrong, but as different opinions.
- We want to make new experiences, so we try to be open to learning.

Personal practice

- The group is focused on creating new brain patterns, so the personal practice that we end each session with is important for you to engage in.
- We will begin each session with a check-in with how your personal practice went, celebrating successes and discussing challenges.

Specific recommendations for the group

_____

_____

_____

Six Core Principles of CFT

1. Genetics	We all have a genetic inheritance we did not choose.
2. Environment	Environment influences the person we have become.
3. Brain	Our brains and emotions are much more difficult to regulate than we think.
4. Responsibility	It is not our fault but it is our responsibility.
5. Compassionate wisdom	The knowledge in principles 1-4 enables us to understand and treat ourselves better.
6. Compassionate cultivation	We can purposefully generate changes in thoughts and feelings.

The Tricky Brain

Flow of Life

Like all living beings, we are part of a greater whole.

1

2

Human Brain

We have a brain we did not design, but which was developed through thousands of years of evolution.

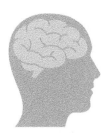 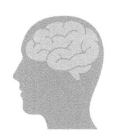

New Brain Capacity

Our brains have the capacity to imagine, have complex language, and be creative—but also the ability to ruminate and worry.

3

Shaped

4

We are shaped by the environment we grew up in, which we did not choose.

Not Your Fault

The brain is tricky because it can get caught in anxious or depressive loops. However, we can take responsibility for it using wisdom and compassion.

5

We Bring the External World into Our Internal World

What we create in our mind will impact our body.

Internal thoughts create internal experiences.

Module 1 Review

Core Content Themes

- The definition of compassion:
  - "Sensitivity to suffering and distress in self and others with a commitment to try to alleviate and prevent it"

- We have a "tricky brain" and are socially constructed
  - We are shaped by genes and life circumstances we did not choose
  - "It's not my fault, but it is my responsibility"

Practice Activities

- Cultivating compassion

Cultivating Compassion

(Note: A digital copy will be provided by your group leader.)

To end this module, we are going to finish with a practice to help you start to cultivate compassion.

We start by closing our eyes or looking down and feeling how we are sitting on our chair right now. (Pause 15 seconds.)

Engage a compassionate posture by having your back straight and shoulders in line with your hips, with an open diaphragm. Now slow your breath, and with each slower and deeper breath say, with a friendly tone, "Mind slowing down," and then "Body slowing down." Alternate these phrases on each out breath. Gradually get that sense of grounding. Gradually feel a sense of stilling and slowing but also with alertness in your mind. Notice yourself becoming more grounded.

Allow time for this to settle in and focus on your breath. (Pause for one minute or so.)

Now tune in to your inner compassionate wisdom. Remember that we all just find ourselves here with a very tricky brain and certain life experiences that have shaped how our minds and bodies work. But we also have a mind that can learn how to change and make choices. So, we are developing the strength and commitment to try to help ourselves and others to deal with life and inner difficulties.

So, as we are sitting here, we also say in a friendly and committed way:

I am coming here today and over the next weeks in order to:

- Work on ways to be helpful to myself (Pause).
- Support others as best I can on their journey (Pause).
- Be open to the helpfulness of others (Pause).

As you feel ready, start to connect with the body in this room again. Feel your body in the chair in this moment, and slowly start to come back into the room. When you are ready, you can open your eyes.

Module 2: Three Systems of Emotion

Aims

- Introduce participants to the three systems of emotion: threat, drive, and soothing.
- Discuss the evolutionary function of these systems and help participants apply this model to their lives.
- Discuss how compassion relates to the three systems.
- Continue soothing rhythm breathing practice and compassionate-self induction.

DOI: 10.4324/9781003202493-3

what is compassion ?

tricky brain

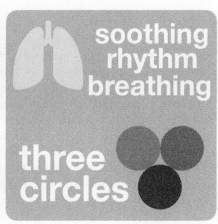

soothing rhythm breathing

three circles

Introduction

In this module, we are going to look at our three emotion systems that evolved to help us survive and thrive. The first is the **threat system**: the system that *helps us deal with things that are potentially dangerous or harmful*. The second is the **drive system**: the system *associated with actively moving towards things that are good for us, and that help us compete and thrive*. The third is the **soothing system**: the system *associated with a sense of peace and relaxation, and feeling connected to the world and other people*. In our group, we will be using the three-circle model (illustrated in Handout 2.1), which identifies the threat system as the "red circle," the drive system as the "blue circle," and the soothing system as the "green circle."

Just because emotions connected with these systems are built in doesn't mean that they are easy to manage. The feelings can be uncomfortable and confusing, and may even interact with each other. For example, we can become angry at our feelings of anxiety, and we can feel frightened of our anger. Emotions are complicated and difficult.

This difficulty sometimes makes us want to get rid of certain emotions. However, all emotions are there to help you survive and thrive—they are important to your existence. We need them. So in this module, we will look at how these emotions play out in our bodies, in our minds, and in our behaviors, and explore ways to develop balance between the three emotion systems.

The red circle represents the threat system, which includes emotions such as anxiety, fear, anger, and disgust. The threat system tells us when we need to be alert. It stimulates our bodies and prepares us for actions that help us stay safe and avoid danger. The threat system is automatic—if you are threatened, your heart rate will go up, even if you'd rather it didn't. If you see a rattle snake, you don't stop to think about what to do next—that could get you killed. This system works very quickly because quick action leads to safety. That's why most people's first instinct is to run. The threat system has its advantages and disadvantages. One major disadvantage is that we tend to notice and remember bad things more than we do good; we attend to threats more quickly, we remember threats more than we remember positives, and we ruminate and hold onto threats. Yet, we must remember that the red circle is also good, because it attempts to keep us safe.

The blue circle is our drive system and includes positive emotions that relate to thriving rather than avoiding danger. Like threat emotions, these positive emotions have an effect on our body, emotions, and attention. Notice that even anticipating having good things happen to you can activate your body. This is important because there are different ways we can activate the body by intentionally choosing what we focus on. Emotions in this system can drive our competitive behavior, and generate behaviors that help us succeed. Sometimes our threat system and our drive system mix, leading to thoughts like, "We can only be happy and have self-worth if we are successful and achieving things." Thus, achievement is motivated by avoiding something negative rather than building something positive. This can make it hard to learn how to cope with the ups and downs of life.

The green circle, or soothing system, is also connected to positive emotions. When animals are not under threat, they can go into a state of restfulness or calming (remember the zebra example). This is an important capacity, because as our body slows down, the mind and body are able to reorganize and recover. Soothing emotions help to balance the other emotions, and they help us to feel safe, explore, and be creative. It activates the higher level functions of the brain that help us make rational decisions. The soothing system can help balance the threat and drive systems. When we're noticing persistent distress, it is likely that this system is being underutilized. Part of developing balance will be practicing activating this soothing system in ways that are most effective. It's important to remember that we don't want to get rid of any of these systems—each of them has an important role. What we want to do is achieve balance between the systems.

When thinking about how our body reacts to the different emotion systems, you may have noticed that some are related to stimulating the body, while others to calming the body. Our **sympathetic nervous system** is the activator—it is threat and drive. Our **parasympathetic system** acts as the brakes—it is soothing. Ideally these two systems should work in balance. Although we're interested in balance, what you may have noticed is that your soothing system isn't working as well as you want. We can concentrate on that and begin to train it—to exercise the soothing system. One way to improve parasympathetic functioning is through soothing rhythm breathing. You can find how to engage in this practice at the end of this module.

The 3 Circle Model & Motivation

Each emotion system is important. Depending on our motivation, our emotion systems will work in different ways.

THREAT (RED) CIRCLE

The threat-focused system is about protection, safety-seeking, and fight/flight. Emotions connected to this system include anger, disgust, fear, and anxiety. The Red Circle is critical to our survival. However, we often let it run the show without realizing it.

DRIVE (BLUE) CIRCLE

The drive system is incentive and resource-focused. It activates us to work toward things we want, desire, or seek to achieve. Emotions connected to this circle are drive, excitement, and vitality. Often we use the Blue Circle to manage our Red Circle emotions.

SOOTHING (GREEN) CIRCLE

The soothing system is about settling, grounding, non-wanting, and safeness. Emotions connected to this circle include being calm and content. It helps us rest and digest, and have open attention. It regenerates us.

COMPETITIVE THREAT

When we have competitive motivation, one characterized by threat, our emotion systems will be unbalanced. Our Red Circles run the show. We can often unknowingly be in this mindset trying to prove our worth to ourselves and others. When in this mindset, we become self-focused and can be very fearful, critical, and hostile towards ourselves and others.

COMPASSIONATE MOTIVE

Our compassionate motive helps restore balance to our emotion systems. Helping us draw on our wisdom, courage, and commitment to be helpful to ourselves and others.

The Function of Anxiety

Threat-Focused

Protection & Safety-Seeking

Activating/Inhibiting

Anxiety

Body/Feelings
* Tense
* Heart rate increase
* Dry mouth
* "Butterflies"
* Afraid

Attention/Thinking
* Narrow-focused
* Danger threat
* Scan/search

Behavior
* Passive avoidance
* Active avoidance
* Submissive display
* Dissociate

Notes:

The Function of Anger

Threat-Focused

Protection & Safety-Seeking

Activating

Anger

Body/Feelings
* Tense
* Heart rate increase
* Pressure to act
* Frustration

Attention/Thinking
* Narrow-focused
* Offense
* Hypervigilance
* Ruminate

Behavior
* Increase outputs
* Aggressive display
* Approach
* Dissociate

Notes:

HANDOUT 2.4

The Function of Drive

Incentive/Resource-Focused
Wanting, Pursuing, Achieving

Consuming, Activating

↓

Excitement/Pleasure

Body/Feelings
* Activation
* Heart rate increase
* Pressure to act
* Disrupt sleep

Attention/Thinking
* Narrow-focused
* Acquiring
* Explorative

Behavior
* Approach
* Engage
* Socialize
* Restless
* Celebrating

Notes:

HANDOUT 2.5

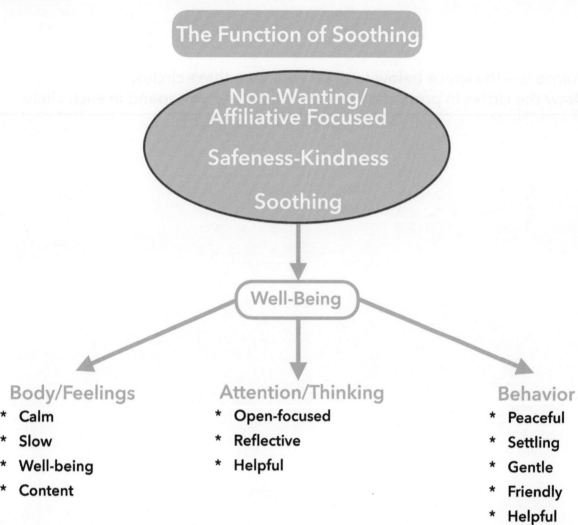

The Function of Soothing

Non-Wanting/Affiliative Focused

Safeness-Kindness

Soothing

Well-Being

Body/Feelings
* Calm
* Slow
* Well-being
* Content

Attention/Thinking
* Open-focused
* Reflective
* Helpful

Behavior
* Peaceful
* Settling
* Gentle
* Friendly
* Helpful

Notes:

Your Own Three Circles

Please use the space below to draw your own three circles.
Draw the circles in proportion to how much time you spend in each circle.

<u>Here are some questions to reflect on:</u>

- What triggers each system for you?
- What keeps you in the zone/system?
- How would you shift to a different emotion system?
- How do soothing and settling help you?

The Natural Balance

The sympathetic system speeds up your heart, and the parasympathetic system slows it down.

Sympathetic System = red & blue
Parasympathetic System = green

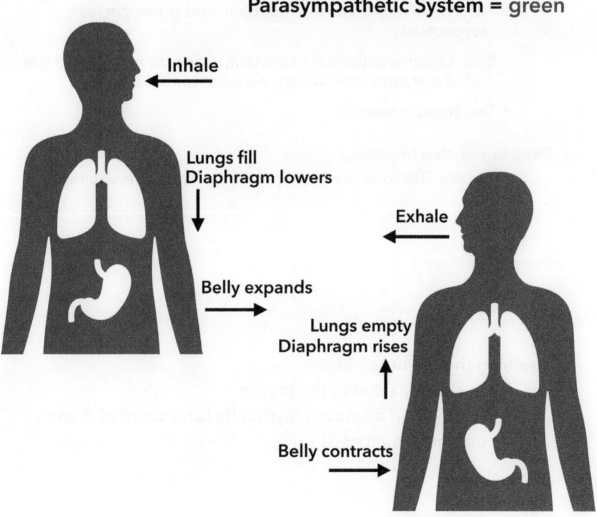

Inhale

Lungs fill
Diaphragm lowers

Belly expands

Exhale

Lungs empty
Diaphragm rises

Belly contracts

Module 2 Review

Core Content Themes

- The three emotion systems
  - Our three emotion systems are threat, drive, and soothing, which we refer to as the red, blue, and green circles, respectively
  - Each of our emotions is important, so we do not want to get rid of any emotions; rather, we want to find balance
  - The Stuart video

- Soothing rhythm breathing
  - We use SRB to activate the parasympathetic nervous system

Practice Activities

- Soothing rhythm breathing
  - We start by slowing the breath
  - We then find a smooth rhythm (in for a count of 5 and out for a count of 5)

Soothing Rhythm Breathing

(Note: A digital copy will be provided by your group leader.)

Let's explore a breathing pattern that can help us be more grounded and feel stable. The idea is just to explore this and see what happens.

Throughout this exercise, see if you can feel relaxed while staying alert. You can allow your eyes to close or, if it's more comfortable for you, you can look gently down at the floor. You may notice that your mind wanders throughout this exercise. If you notice it happening, that's okay. That's part of what minds do. Just notice it when it happens, give it a label (I was thinking about that assignment I have due), and gently bring your mind back to my voice, to this exercise, and to your breathing.

First, notice your posture:

1 Lift your shoulders up and back. The threat system curls your posture inwards. So here, we are deliberately unfolding the body into a more confident, open posture.
2 Try to get your ears in line with your shoulders, and your shoulders in line with your hips.
3 Allow yourself to breath into your diaphragm.

Take a moment to just notice your natural breath. Notice the air coming in and out through your nose in a relatively easy way—don't try to change your breathing at all or make it deeper. Just in gently and out gently—in gently and out gently. Notice how the air comes down into your lungs and then out again, like a wave coming in and out of the shore. Focus on finding a rhythm that feels comfortable to you. See what it's like just to sit with an open posture, focusing on your breath. Notice this on your own for a few moments.

(Pause 30 seconds.)

Now let's work on slightly changing that natural rhythm to help activate your parasympathetic system, or the "brakes" we were talking about. See if you can begin to slow and deepen your natural breath—lengthen your rhythm. We're going to be aiming for about 5 seconds in and 5 seconds out.

There are two parts to the exercise of soothing rhythm breathing: the first part is slowing the breath, and the second part is the smoothness of the breath—allowing yourself to gently breathe in and out in a smooth rhythm.

For some, counting in 5 seconds and out 5 seconds can be helpful. For others, that can get in the way. Find what works best for you as you continue to try to slow and smooth your breathing. When you breathe out, let it be a gentle, smooth exhale rather than forcing the air out. Let it leave slowly and naturally. It can sometimes help to attend to just the out breath—the air leaving your nose with a steady rhythm.

As you develop your rhythm, notice and focus on the feeling of inner slowing with each out breath. You might say on each out breath with a friendly, supportive, internal voice:

Body Slowing Down (Say slowly, at a pace of about 5 seconds.)

And you might alternate that with:

Mind Slowing Down (Say slowly, at a pace of about 5 seconds.)

Allow these three words to stretch across your full out breath.

Try to notice how your body responds to your breathing. Try to connect with a rhythm that is soothing and calming to you. See if this can become more than just the rhythm of your breathing—see if it can expand to a more complete inner rhythm.

Try to practice this for 1 minute on your own. Before we do this, remember that it is normal for your mind to wander. Simply notice it happening and then gently guide your attention back to an awareness of your body breathing steadily in and out; just noticing the flow of air coming in and out of your nose. Try to just gently observe things as they are. Notice your mind slowing down; your body slowing down.

Now let's try 1 minute. You can continue to count for yourself, if that is helpful, or just notice the experience of smoothly and evenly breathing in and breathing out.

(Pause 60 seconds.)

Notice the feeling of slowing and grounding. Notice that you may now feel slightly heavier in the chair. Allow yourself to sink into the chair and let the chair hold you up. Sense this body awareness. (Pause) This is called grounding. Sense the weight of your body resting on the chair and the floor underneath you. Notice how your body may feel slightly heavier in the chair now that you have slowed your breath. Allow yourself to feel held and supported—coming to rest in the present moment—staying alert with good body posture. Feel the stableness in your body that has come from the slowing of the breath. Imagine sitting like a mountain, strong and stable.

See if you can sense your capacity for inner stillness—like the calmness of a lake or a tree—still, without wind. You might notice that you feel only slightly more still rather than feeling very still. That's normal. Think of it as part of moving in the direction of slowing, stilling, and grounding.

Now start to let go of the practice of soothing rhythm breathing. Start to come back slowly into the room, noticing your body in the chair, feet on the ground, the sounds in the room. And when you feel ready, open your eyes.

Module 3: Mindfulness

Aims

- Help group members understand that they can direct and be intentional with their attention.
- Introduce mindfulness and help group members practice it.
- Help group members notice the effects of attention and its power to affect our experiences.
- Help group members notice the effect of body posture, internal vocal tone, and emotion labeling on their internal experiences.
- Help group members apply all of the concepts discussed (mindfulness, body posture, vocal tone, and emotion labeling, along with soothing rhythm breathing) to a difficult situation.

DOI: 10.4324/9781003202493-4

what is compassion ?

tricky brain

soothing rhythm breathing

three circles

focused attention

mindfulness

Introduction

This module is designed to help us learn how to *focus what our brain attends to*—kind of like a search- or spotlight illuminates what it shines upon. Most brains go through a cycle of attending and, just like the three-circle model, we'll introduce a model of mindfulness to help you become more aware of your own attending process. What we attend to can help us or become problematic.

Attention is like a flashlight—when you focus your attention on something, you shine your mental "flashlight" onto it. So, while we focus on some things in our mind, other things fall out of mind. They are still there, you have just stopped being aware of them (like no longer noticing the fan or the air conditioner). To notice where your attention is, you may ask yourself, "Where is my attention pointing?" or "Where is my mind pointing?" You are in charge of where your attention is directed. We can **shift** attention not only to our surroundings or the current moment, but also towards our memories of the past, emotions, and thoughts. When we shift our attention, our body and mind change accordingly. For example, remember a moment when you were having fun with a friend; you were laughing or simply having a great time. Notice the feelings in your body when you move your attention to this joyful moment. Then recall a moment when you were having a little argument with someone, maybe even the same person. Notice the feelings in your body when you move your attention to this difficult moment. Because our bodies and minds are influenced by where we direct our attention, being caught (or stuck) in our threat system can cause a lot of stress. We might need to practice noticing what is happening internally and increasing compassion towards what we are focused on using breathing, grounding, and compassion intention.

Sometimes, we go into "automatic pilot." When we are in "automatic pilot," we do not pay attention, or we may fail to act with intent. Some examples of automatic pilot are driving home without really remembering, getting angry and acting out in angry ways that you might later regret, feeling hungry and then eating food you regret, etc. **Mindfulness** is the way of breaking into that link by becoming aware so that we begin to make choices with intent. For example, I may feel angry but I don't behave destructively. Mindfulness helps us keep to our intention because it helps us keep intention in mind. Handouts 3.1 and 3.2 are meant to help you better understand and explore mindfulness.

One mindfulness skill that can help us stay in the moment is **emotion labeling**. Emotion labeling, or naming an emotion, helps us become calm and less entangled with the emotion. We practice emotion labeling to ensure that our emotions are *not* running the show. Instead, we want to make sure that we are in charge; we want to act with intent. Emotions can be rapidly and intensely triggered and, if not mindful, we then may think and act from that position. Using mindfulness and emotion labeling, we are able to decide how we actually want to act; we become a wise actor rather than a reactor.

In the last module, we discussed how the three types of emotion (*threat*, *drive*, and *soothing*) are associated with certain body postures, emotions, and physical reactions. Our body posture, voice tone, and facial expression impact our internal world, and we therefore want to be aware of them. We can create compassionate body postures that help put us into a compassionate state by becoming aware and observant of our body postures and states. Doing so helps us prepare the body for compassion and more regularly switch into it.

Let's experiment for a minute with how our body posture, facial expressions, and voice tones can affect our emotions. Let your body curl inwards and drop forward as if you had a depressed posture. Then, think to yourself: "*No, I can't.*" What does that feel like? Now sit upright as if you are in a very confident position, your shoulders back in line with your hips, and your head up with a slight friendly smile on your face. Say in your mind in a very friendly voice: "*Yes, I can,*" and repeat this a few times with a gentle smile on your face. What does that feel like? To explore how powerful facial expressions can be, first just sit with your soothing rhythm breathing with a neutral facial expression for 5–10 seconds. Then create a gentle smile and a friendly facial expression, and try to create a feeling of friendliness in your face. Imagine you are with a friend and you are showing them with your friendly face that you are pleased to see them. Just notice how creating facial expressions can change feelings you have, even if only just a small bit or just slightly. Now let's explore voice tones—neutral and friendly. Continuing your soothing rhythm breathing, on the out breath, say to yourself: "*Hello [say your name].*" Say this in a neutral voice tone for 5 seconds and then in a friendly tone for 5 seconds. Note how your voice tone is linked to your emotions.

When we first try using body posture, voice tone, and facial expressions to prepare our bodies for compassion, it can feel strange and artificial. However, the more we practice, the better we get and the more natural this will feel. The subtle changes in body posture, tone, and facial expression impact the way that we relate to ourselves and the way we relate to the world around us.

Cycle of Mindfulness

Mindfulness is a practice of noticing and gently returning to the moment—not trying to rid one's mind of thoughts. It helps us to become aware of what's going on in our minds and to bring our minds where we want them to be.

Mindfulness Exercises

Mindful Breathing

This Mindful Breathing exercise involves pausing, watching our breath, and noticing when our attention leaves our breath (e.g., getting lost in thoughts, becoming distracted by a sensation inside or outside ourselves, getting caught up in an emotion, etc.).

HOW TO DO IT:

• First, sit comfortably. Place your feet shoulder-width apart, flat on the ground. If you don't have anywhere to sit comfortably, then lying down is all right. The point is to be physically comfortable, but not to fall asleep. You might like to close your eyes if you feel comfortable doing so, or otherwise you can find a spot on the wall or ground to focus on throughout the exercise.

• Now **gently focus your attention on your breath**. Breathe so that the air enters your diaphragm—just at the bottom of your ribcage. Notice your abdomen rising and falling as you breathe in and out. Just notice your breath for about 30 seconds.

• If you're like most of us, your mind probably wandered away fairly quickly. You may have had thoughts like, "How is this supposed to help me?" or "I'm hungry. I can't wait to eat." Or maybe, "Am I doing this right?"

• **The idea is to just watch your breath, and begin to notice when your attention drifts off. When you notice that your attention has left your breath, just gently bring it back to your breath, again and again, over and over.**

• **The fact that your attention wanders off is not a problem**. In fact, a major point of this exercise is to learn to notice when you have thoughts and feelings, and are distracted by sensations. Actually, **we need for our attention to wander, so that we can learn to notice when thoughts and feelings pop up.**

• **The key is that when our thoughts and emotions come up, we don't judge them...we just notice them as mental events ("Oh... there's another thought") and then come back to the breath.**

Mindful Eating

• You can try this when eating an apple or anything else.

• If you are eating an apple, pay attention to the fruit's texture.

• Note the food's (in this case apple) texture using your fingers, then smell it, and then take a bite. Take time to experience each of these sensations. Feel the food in your mouth to explore its texture.

• Try to see if you can notice how different the food's texture is with your fingers compared with your mouth.

• You can then explore its taste and slowly swallow.

• Try to explore the sense of swallowing and the sense of where the food has gone in your body.

• This is called mindful eating because it's paying attention, on purpose, and in the present moment, to the act of eating.

Mindful Walking

• You can also do mindful walking. In this exercise, just go for a walk; it could be in your room or outside.

• Just try to simply walk mindfully around the room, footpath, or garden mindfully noticing objects, picking them up, and exploring them.

• If you are in the garden, notice your surroundings (trees, flowers, smells, temperature, sounds, etc.). Try to use as many senses as you can.

• The idea is to learn to be immersed in the activity itself; not thinking about the activity.

Other Ways to be Mindful

• Painting or drawing.

• Listening to music.

• Watching sand pass through a bottle.

• Watching the waves of the ocean or clouds in the sky.

Notes:

_____

_____

_____

_____

Starting the Day with Compassion

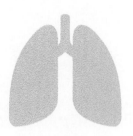

BREATHE

Engage in soothing rhythm breathing. That means keeping an evenness between the in-breath and out-breath. Try a count of 4 for in and a count of 4 for out. Focus on keeping the out-breath smooth.

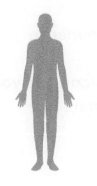

WELCOME YOURSELF

Welcome yourself to the day like you would a dear friend. You might like to bring a half-smile to your face and use your friendly tone.

IMAGINE

Imagine for 1–2 minutes how your day will look if you are at your compassionate best. How would you talk? How would you respond to others? How would you act? How would you feel?

REPEAT

Try to repeat every third morning to begin with. Then, slowly start to build to every other day. Finally, do it every day. When we welcome ourselves in this way, we are giving ourselves the best chance to be at our compassionate best.

Module 3 Review

Core Content Themes

- Attention and mindfulness
  - Attention as a "flashlight"
  - When we are mindful, we act with intent
  - Cycle of mindfulness

- Body posture, facial expressions, and voice tones
  - What happens externally impacts what we experience internally
  - A compassionate body posture, facial expressions, and voice tones can help put us into a compassionate state

Practice Activities

- Applying mindfulness to a difficult situation

Applying Mindfulness to a Difficult Situation

(Note: A digital copy will be provided by your group leader.)

Let's see what happens if we apply all of these ideas to a small life difficulty. For example, getting places on time, figuring out what we're talking about, or going to the store and forgetting to buy something we needed. Try to avoid major difficulties right now—we want to ease into it. What small difficulties can you think of?

Let's begin by trying to get comfortable. Go ahead and sit upright, and gently close your eyes. If you prefer, just direct your gaze downwards.

Bring to mind a slightly negative event that you have experienced recently, again, nothing too extreme or heavy, but something that was a slight disappointment or annoyance for you. Just bring it to mind. Let your body take the posture that it naturally takes when you are thinking about that negative event or disappointment. So, for example, if it is disappointment, your shoulders might drop and curl.

Become aware of your own inner dialogue, both the content and tone of your voice, while you are thinking about the event. Notice what you are saying, how you are saying it, how you are feeling in your body, and what your body posture feels like.

Just notice this and observe it mindfully. (Pause)

How would you label your state now? Slightly tense? Anxious? Irritable? (Pause)

Now we're going to start deliberately switching our mental state as best we can. We are going to try to think of this same problem through the mind and body pattern of the compassionate-self and see what happens.

As you keep thinking of this negative event, I want you to gently move into and assume your compassionate body posture. Feet flat on the floor, sitting upright. Lift your shoulders and move them backward slightly. When you do this, notice that your chest opens up and that your back curves slightly. Make sure your head is in an upright position.

Now relax your face and see if you can shift it into a friendlier facial expression. See if you can replace any angry or negative vocal tones with friendlier ones.

And now, just slow down your breathing a little. Just settle your mind and body. Remember, you can either count the seconds so you are breathing in for about 5 seconds and out for about 5 seconds, or if counting gets in your way, just slow your breathing to a comfortable, slow rhythm. When you breathe out, let your breath be a gentle, smooth exhale.

As you develop this natural rhythm, focus on the feeling of inner slowing with each out breath. Say on each alternate out breath in a friendly, supportive voice:

Mind Slowing Down
Body Slowing Down

When you say these words, say them slowly. Each word should take longer to say—until the three words basically use up the 5 seconds.

Let's practice that for one minute. You can continue to count for yourself if that is helpful, or just notice the experience of smoothly and evenly breathing in and breathing out. (1 minute)

Now that we have developed this compassionate posture, notice a sense of stability, of being firm and grounded, like a mountain. If you aren't feeling this yet, don't worry—grounding yourself can be a difficult process, and it takes time to figure it out. Just remember your intention to develop a more compassionate, helpful, friendly self.

With this mind, let's revisit the negative event or disappointment you brought to mind at the beginning of this exercise. Let's spend a moment really thinking about this difficulty through a more compassionate sense of self, with a more open posture, a friendlier facial expression, and a kinder vocal tone. Try to label the emotions you're noticing. Again, don't worry if your mind wanders or if you find it difficult. The idea is simply to try it out and see what happens. (Pause for at least one minute.)

And now, just let that experience go, and slowly come back into the room.

Let's reflect on your experience. What did you notice?

Module 4: Feeling Safe and Receiving Compassion from Others

Aims

- Help group members understand the difference between feeling safe in an environment and feeling threatened in an environment.
- Discuss the importance of creating an internal secure base.
- Practice imagery to create an internal safe-space.
- Discuss the importance and difficulty of receiving compassion from others.
- Practice ideal compassionate other imagery.

DOI: 10.4324/9781003202493-5

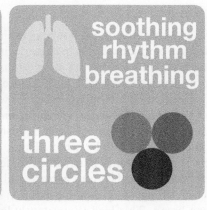

Introduction

The last few modules have explored ways of thinking about how our brains, emotions, and past experiences affect daily life. You'll remember that we have emotions that help us deal with threats (red circle), emotions that motivate us to go out and achieve (blue circle), and another set of emotions that are linked to feeling safe and relaxed (green circle). Compassion helps us learn to work with and balance these emotions. We have looked at how we can use our bodies, particularly posture and breathing, to help us with difficult emotions.

In this module, *we are going to look at the ideas of the inner safe place, and explore what it means to feel safe.*

When we feel **threatened**, we are looking to stop bad things from happening. Attention is constantly on the lookout for the next possible threat. Sometimes, this can be useful. Think back to the circles—the concept of feeling threatened is based in the red circle. On the other hand, when we feel safe, we can relax and enjoy our surroundings, take pleasure from where we are, and begin to explore and try new things; we can be playful. **Safety** is much more focused in the green soothing and grounding emotion system.

Imagine a bird on a lawn eating some bread. This bird is constantly looking for potential threats, and if any threat is noticed, the bird flies away very quickly; better safe than sorry. So the bird is unlikely to savor and enjoy the bread. This bird is feeling threatened. Compare this to animals that are pets, or animals at a national park that have been exposed to numerous people feeding them. They are able to enjoy the food they are eating because of a sense of safety. Trusting that we are safe is what makes us feel safe in our environment. Experiencing safety is part of the healing process, and we can recreate an "inner safe base." Take a minute and think about what you need to allow yourself to feel safe enough to take risks and develop in the ways you want. What are your typical safety strategies—the things you do to try to prevent bad things from happening?

One way in which we can better feel a sense of safety is through **imagery**. Imagery is a way to stimulate systems in our bodies that can be very useful to us. As we have seen before, how we stimulate our minds can have an impact on our bodies. This is why it's so important to create secure and compassionate imagery; it helps build our parasympathetic (or "soothing") system.

One of the common concerns that people have with imagery is that they will not be able to generate or create a clear picture in their mind. This is perfectly normal, as we rarely have clear pictures in our mind. Images tend to be more like fleeting impressions—a touch of color here, or a sense of something there. Often times, imagining hearing things can be easier, especially imagining people speaking to us. Again, **the clarity of imagery is not as important as the act of trying to imagine**. We aren't creating perfect polaroid pictures in the mind, just fleeting images. For example, what is a bicycle? What is an elephant? What did you have for breakfast? The only reason you are able to answer these questions is because your mind flashes an image for each. The images do not need to be perfectly clear, just good enough to give a sense. At the end of this module are two imagery exercises, Safe Place Imagery and Ideal Compassionate Other, which are provided to help you feel more safety and compassion.

Another important concept in this module is the Interactive Flow of Compassion (Handout 4.2). There are *different flows of compassion: compassion from others, compassion to others,* and *self-compassion.* An easy way to remember this is that there are two flows in, and one flow out; self-compassion and compassion from others (in), and then compassion to others (out).

Let's focus on *compassion from others.* Allowing compassion from others is important. From the day we are born, we need others to feed us, comfort us, and care for us in order to survive—this is the way that our brains are set up. Our species would not survive otherwise. Being cared for has the same importance as food. Sadly, and tragically, we sometimes don't get the care or attention we need. This can leave us feeling angry, anxious, sad, or distrusting, and tends to lead toward a desire to pull for more support or push people away. Our tricky brains can be uncomfortable with receiving compassion if we have not received or allowed ourselves to receive compassion from others in the past, usually as a result of being in the threat system and a state of safety seeking. Again, this is not our fault, but it is our responsibility. As we learn to accept compassion from others, we can begin to reclaim what nature has given us and we can feel more understood, less lonely, and less likely to rely solely on ourselves for the support we all need.

One way for us to tune into compassion from others is to just *remember a time when others were helpful.* Go ahead and settle into soothing rhythm breathing for a moment. Slow your breath and access your compassionate-self.

Now, bring to mind somebody in your life who has been helpful...somebody to whom you have felt grateful. Try not to focus on the distress that you were feeling, but rather on the positive feelings of gratitude to the other person, no matter how small. If you were able to talk with that person right now, what would you like to say and why would you like to say what you would? If you were to write a letter to them, what would you want to write? What was it like being able to accept care from this person? What did you notice about resistances to accepting compassion from others? What did you notice about your ability to accept care without feeling the need to repay?

Safety vs. Threat

FEELING THREATENED

- We are focused on threat and look to stop bad things from happening. This makes good sense, but constantly checking for threats can stop us from doing what we want or need to do.

- For example, if we go rock climbing, we wear a harness to prevent the threat of falling, but we don't tie into the rope and leave the ground.

VS.

- Safety focuses on creating the conditions to allow us to explore our surroundings and gives us courage to explore things we might fear or worry about.
- With a feeling of safety comes the freedom to explore, being open to experience and enabling growth, development, and flourishing.
- A feeling of safety allows us to go rock climbing knowing we are secure in our harness.

FEELING SAFE

The Interactive Flow of Compassion

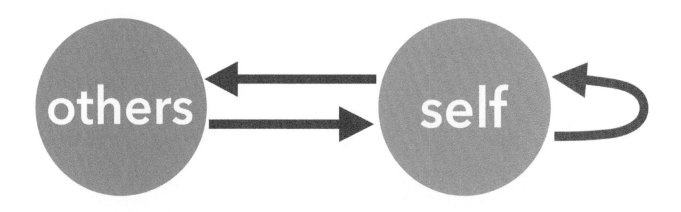

*Each has its own facilitators and inhibitors.

Building the Compassionate Image

This is an opportunity for you to describe everything you would want from a compassionate other.

How would you like your ideal compassionate caring image to appear? They can be humanlike or nonhuman—the more detail you give them, the easier it will be to feel connected. Are they by your side, or in front of you? Remember, you may not have clear images, rather, just a sense of something.

How does your ideal compassionate other sound (e.g., the volume and texture of their voice)?

What other qualities would you like them to have (e.g., is it peaceful, firm, enveloping, flexible)?

How would you like this compassionate image to relate to you?

How would you like to relate to your compassionate image?

Module 4 Review

Core Content Themes

- Safety vs. threat

- Imagery
    - Imagery as a tool to feel security
    - You do not need a perfectly clear image

- The three flows of compassion: compassion from others, compassion to others, and self-compassion

Practice Activities

- Safe place imagery

- Ideal compassionate other

Safe Place Imagery

(Note: A digital copy will be provided by your group leader.)

So, let's think about what it would be like to be in a place that could allow you to feel completely safe. Think what you might like to do if you felt secure in this place. Before getting too far into this safe place, let's take a minute to engage our compassionate-self, as this will help in the imagery process. Gently close your eyes or cast your gaze to the ground. Take up your compassionate body position of shoulders back and chest open, a slight inward curve in the back, and the breathing at around five breaths per minute. Allow yourself to obtain a sense of grounding. Really try to focus on having a friendly voice and friendly facial expression. (Pause for about 30 seconds.)

Now, when you're ready, see if you can bring to mind a place that could let you feel okay, comfortable, calm, and ideally some degree of security.

If this is difficult for you, simply think of a type of place that you would like to be—that is, if given a choice, a place you would prefer to be. Think about a place where you feel comfortable. Start simple. This may be a new experience for you. Remember that there is no right or wrong way of doing this. This is just a way of exploring our minds a little bit and seeing what happens. This is part of something called guided discovery. So, if possible, see if you can engage in this activity with a sense of playfulness and curiosity. Really allow yourself to see what emerges. (Pause)

Think about the following: Would you prefer a place that is inside or outside? What is the weather like? Is it night or day? Is the air around you warm or cold?

Now consider some details of your safe place. Are you somewhere where there are trees, or by a sea, or up a mountain, or in a nice garden? What is the texture of the light; is it dark or clear and sunny?

If you're indoors, check in with your mind to see if you are there because that allows you to feel comfortable, or if you are there because you'd be frightened or worried about going out. There is nothing wrong with being indoors if you are afraid of going out…just recognize that this is the case in a non-judgmental way. Indeed, sometimes when we're tired, we can just imagine how nice it would be to get back home to bed and snuggle up with that warm relief sort of feeling. Sleep, as a secure place, is interesting because we have to attend to our safety before sleep, and that's often why we like to be hidden away when we sleep. As much as you can, allow this secure place to be a place where you are not trying to escape anything, but where you really feel like you can just be, where you feel free to explore and be playful.

Next, imagine the kind of sounds that might be around you. Again, just have a general sense of what sorts of sounds might be there and what sounds you would like, if any. (Pause)

Imagine if there are any other sensations for you. What are you walking on? If you are barefoot in your secure place, how does the ground feel beneath your feet? What might you want to touch or hold? (Pause)

Notice if you can smell anything in your secure space. If you could smell something in this place, what would you like to smell? Is it the freshness of the air, the smell of the ocean, flowers? Just take a moment and notice. (Pause)

Now we are going to imagine our relationship to our secure place. We can start by what might seem like a strange thing to imagine—see if you can experience this secure place as welcoming you. For a moment, imagine that everything around you welcomes you. You have created this image in your mind, so it's part of you; connected to you. Creating this feeling of being welcome is very good for our brains. So try to imagine that the place itself takes joy in you being there. For example, if there are clouds above you, they enjoy you being there. If there are trees around you, they take delight in you walking around. They make you feel welcomed; like you belong here with them. It's your place, created by you and for you. Explore your feelings when you imagine that this place is happy you are there. Even if it is just a fleeting sense, create a facial expression of friendliness and openness as you imagine being welcomed. Allow yourself to have a soft smile of pleasure at being there. Remember the friendly voice tone that we practiced last week. (Pause)

Now we're going to look at the concept of freedom and exploration, which can also be helpful for our brains. Think about what you would like to do in this safe place. Just let your mind come up with anything it wants. If nothing occurs to you, that's okay too. Sometimes it's nice not to do anything but relax and feel a sense of belonging. Whatever arises is okay if it works for you.

Feel free to be creative in any way you want. For example, maybe you'd like to take a leisurely walk, cycle, run, climb a mountain, fly, or swim underwater without needing to come up for air. Anything goes. The only rule that ever applies in this secure place is that your image should not involve causing harm to yourself or other living things.

You may notice that as you think about doing things in your safe place, it may change around you. This is to be expected and commonly happens. If your mind wants it to change, don't try to hold onto only one image of this place. Again, the idea is just to allow your mind to play because you feel safe and secure. (Pause)

Now slowly start letting that image fade, come back into the room, and notice how your body feels in your chair. When you are ready, open your eyes.

Ideal Compassionate Other

(Note: A digital copy will be provided by your group leader.)

We are now going to build on our intuitive wisdom to create the image of a compassionate other. The ideal other is not necessarily a person. It could be an animal, like a lion or bear that protects, or it could be a strong and rooted tree. Whatever works for you is fine to start with. Just as you might have at one time imagined your ideal parent, friend, lover, or business partner, we can use this imagination to create an ideal compassionate other. The images of the compassionate other we create can help to stimulate our brains toward a more compassionate way of being.

So go ahead and gently close your eyes, or cast your gaze towards the ground. We're just going to start to imagine our ideal compassionate other. This compassionate other is wise, kind, helpful, and insightful. They will have perfect compassionate wisdom, strength, and commitment. Ideal means that the compassionate other doesn't have to suffer from human fallibility, weakness, or bad habits. It is exactly what you would want; even if it's unrealistic. The act of creating this other is what is important for our minds.

Maybe start by thinking about appearance. As I said before, sometimes people prefer not to think about humans, but may think of a plant, animal, or object. The key to creating this compassionate other is that it has its own mind that completely understands the human condition. It understands that we have tricky brains, and that we can suffer and get caught in loops with our own minds. See what emerges for you. Different people have different ideals. Take a moment to consider the following:

- Would you want your ideal compassionate other to have a gender? If so, what gender would you prefer?
- What is the age of your ideal compassionate other? Older? Younger? The same age?
- What sort of size would this ideal compassionate other be?
- Do you have any sense of facial expressions?
- If they have hair or eyes, do you have an impression of hair color or eye color? Remember you don't need to see anything clearly, just an impression.
- If they have clothing, how might they be clothed? (Pause)

Next, we can start to think about how they communicate with you. What sort of friendly voice tone would you like for this compassionate other to have? Again, you do not need to have a clear picture of this. Allow a sense of this to be enough.

Once you have a sense of this compassionate other, think of the qualities you would like for it to have.

To help you, here are some ideas that people typically want from a compassionate other: patience, tolerance, wisdom, friendliness, gentleness, openness, understanding, strength, determination, playfulness, humor, easy to be with. What other qualities would you want it to have? (Pause)

Try to turn this image into one that you would like to be with and feel comfortable with. If you don't feel comfortable with the image, then play around with it until it has the qualities you'd like, so that you are comfortable with it. Your ideal compassionate other is not distant or beyond you. It is understanding and shares wisdom with you, with the complete intention of addressing your suffering and helping in any way it can. The ideal compassionate-other certainly does not cause suffering in any way. Take a moment to really think about your compassionate other and the characteristics it has. (Pause 60–90 seconds.)

Now that we have created an image of an ideal compassionate other, we are going to imagine relating to it. As always, keep this relatively open and playful rather than too intense.

Let's see how we can use this image with a small life difficulty or life challenge you are dealing with. Nothing too major, but something that you are disappointed about or that causes you some anxiety, irritation, or frustration. Bring this small life difficulty to mind. (Pause)

And now imagine that you are with your ideal compassionate other, with its wisdom, strength and authority, and commitment toward helping you through your suffering. Remember the other qualities this ideal compassionate other has, such as patience, understanding, kindness, eagerness to help. How would you like your ideal compassionate other to relate to you with this life difficulty? Think about the following questions:

- What voice tone would you hear? Would it be friendly? Understanding?
- How might this ideal compassionate other help you think about your past coping efforts? What would it say of your strengths and struggles?
- What kind of reassuring voice would it offer?
- How would you feel best understood?

- How might it help you remember your own wisdom that we all just find ourselves here working through our struggles as best we can?
- How would you like to relate to your image?
- What kind of things would you want to say to this image?
- Remembering that you can say anything you want about anything you want, what concerns would you like to share? (Pause)

Now slowly start letting that image fade, coming back into the room, and noticing how your body feels in your chair. When you are ready, open your eyes.

Module 5: Compassionate-Self

Aims

- Introduce group members to the nature and concept of compassionate-self.
- Point out how different self-identities occur and how we can train and cultivate the compassionate-self.
- Activate the compassionate-self.

DOI: 10.4324/9781003202493-6

what is compassion

tricky brain

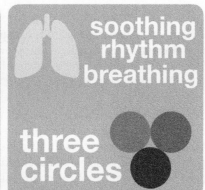
soothing rhythm breathing

three circles

focused attention

mindfulness

feeling safe

other selves

compassionate-self

Introduction

The focus of this module will be on building our compassionate-self. **Compassion is having a sensitivity to pain and suffering in self and others with a commitment to try to relieve and prevent it.** There are many qualities to compassion, but in compassion focused therapy we focus on the three qualities of 1) *wisdom*, 2) *strength*, and 3) *commitment*. These make what we call **The Compassionate-Self**. We will be working through these today looking at each of them.

To begin exploring your compassionate-self, bring to mind a memory of when you wanted to help somebody who was struggling. As you think back on this time, what were you paying attention to? What were you thinking? How did it feel in your body? How did you want to act? As this exercise shows, you already have intuitive wisdom about what it means to be compassionate. It is possible to develop a compassionate-self because: (a) we have this intuitive wisdom, and (b) we have power to cultivate the compassionate way of being by approaching it intentionally.

Compassion is just another way of being, among many other ways of being. We can practice to become better at being in a compassionate state, much like how muscles are already there but they get stronger and serve us better if we intentionally exercise. Part of exercising compassion is being more committed to avoiding intentional or careless harm to oneself or to others.

Think back on our first few modules when we talked about how we didn't choose all of our environment or the body we were born into, and how if we had been born into a very different environment, we may be very different people. Even in everyday life, we are different in different situations—we are not just one thing, but we are multiple things. Think about all of the different emotions you've had over the last week. Was there a time, even a brief time, when you felt happy? Anxious? Sad? Scared? Peaceful? The point is, there is variation of and in our current state of being, even if it feels like the bulk of our experience is around negative emotions.

Given that we shift from one thing to another, let's reflect on things that can evoke these emotions—like watching a movie or hearing a story. These are largely entertaining because we feel something that we wouldn't have otherwise—the entertainment shifts our state, even if it's just for a moment. Can you think of what creates shifts in your emotional experience (even brief shifts) for you? Some examples could be talking to a friend, going for a walk, or meditating.

Now think about our exercises with mindfulness—where we talked about being able to choose where we put the "flashlight" of our attention. We're going to try to merge these two ideas—that you have multiple selves that you shift between, and that you have the power to choose a focus— to help develop our compassionate state of mind and compassionate-self.

So let's start by just imagining a compassionate state of mind and a compassionate-self. What would this be like? What qualities would it have? It may be helpful to look at Handout 5.1 to consider the qualities of a compassionate-self.

Once you have a good idea of what your compassionate-self would look like, try to step into it. It might be helpful to imagine that you are an actor who has been given the part to play a very compassionate person. Sometimes people think of someone they know who is deeply compassionate and then imagine what it would be like to become like them—to try to see the world through their eyes, with their intentions and their behaviors. Don't worry about whether you can be compassionate or not; try to allow yourself to just experiment with this and notice what it's like. You may find it helpful to try the meditation "Activating the Compassionate-Self" provided at the end of this module, which is meant to help you access your compassionate-self. Then, to end, let's practice applying our compassionate-self to our own lives by going through Handout 5.2.

Notes on Domains of Wisdom, Strength, & Commitment

WISDOM

- We all have a genetic inheritance we did not choose
- Our environments influenced the people we have become
- Our brains and emotions are much more difficult to regulate than we think
- It is not our fault but it is our responsibility
- These are common to **all** of us

INNER AUTHORITY AND STRENGTH

- Authority grows from wisdom
- I can develop this through:
  - Mindfulness
  - Upright posture (anchored on the ground below with a sense of support)
  - Facial expressions of friendliness
  - An awareness of body
- It is my responsibility to practice these skills

COURAGE AND COMMITMENT TO...

- Gain insight into the nature of things
- Pay attention to needs for compassion
- Build courage to turn towards suffering
- Build a self who wishes to avoid causing harm
- Develop the competencies for compassionate action
- Dedicate to find ways to be helpful and prevent suffering
- Practice for a compassionate mind to grow and develop
- See the benefits to self and others

A Compassionate-Self Response

Think about a difficult situation, but nothing that causes too much distress. As best as you can, write some thoughts and beliefs that your usual self would have. For example: *"I can't handle situations like this, I get too emotional,"* or something similar. Then, change roles: activate your compassionate-self and respond.

My "threat/worried/upset self" thinks:

1. _____
2. _____
3. _____
4. _____

My "compassionate-self" thinks:

1. _____
2. _____
3. _____
4. _____

My "threat/worried/upset self" does:

1. _____
2. _____
3. _____
4. _____

My "compassionate-self" does:

1. _____
2. _____
3. _____
4. _____

My "threat/worried/upset self" wants:

1. _____
2. _____
3. _____
4. _____

My "compassionate-self" wants:

1. _____
2. _____
3. _____
4. _____

How I feel now (as my worried-self):

1. _____
2. _____
3. _____
4. _____

How I feel now (as my compassionate-self):

1. _____
2. _____
3. _____
4. _____

Module 5 Review

Core Content Themes

- Self-compassion
  - Compassionate-self as being compassionate; compassionate mind as having a compassionate point of view for yourself and others
  - Self-compassion is made possible by our innate wisdom of and commitment to compassion
  - Stepping into the compassionate-self

- Three qualities of compassion: wisdom, strength/authority, and commitment

Practice Activities

- Activating the compassionate-self

Activating the Compassionate-Self

(Note: A digital copy will be provided by your group leader.)

Let's start with grounding ourselves first and getting into a physical state that more easily allows for compassion. Try to notice:

- Feeling grounded; feeling heavier in the chair; sitting firm and stable, like a mountain.
- Compassionate breath that's slower and more open, using your diaphragm.
- Compassionate posture, with shoulders back and back straight, relaxed but alert.
- Compassionate facial expression.
- Compassionate inner voice tone.

Now take a moment to try to step into your compassionate-self—step into all those qualities that we listed on the board. What does it feel like to be that kind of compassionate person? What kind of thoughts do you have? What kind of feelings? What kind of behaviors? What intentions do you have? Take a moment to try to really imagine what it would be like to be this perfectly compassionate self. If you notice that you're having difficulty, just notice this difficulty, and then gently bring your attention back to what it would be like to be your perfectly compassionate self. See if you can feel it in your mind and your body.

Now think of the three qualities of compassion: wisdom, strength and authority, and commitment.

Let's first attend to the quality of **wisdom**. Remind yourself that you have the wisdom that we all just find ourselves here with a tricky brain that we didn't choose. At times it can be chaotic, tricky, and painful—and this isn't your fault. You have this wisdom right now, and you understand other people are like that, too.

You also have the wisdom of how you've coped with things in your life thus far, as well as the intuitive compassion that you feel when those you care about need help. You have wisdom, in this moment, that you can build on.

Now attend to the quality of **strength and authority**. As you ground yourself with your breathing, sitting upright in your chair, notice your sense of groundedness and strength. Notice how that feels in your body and your mind. You have the ability to feel, to some degree, strong and grounded.

Now attend to the quality of **commitment**. See if you can feel committed to your compassionate motivation. Can you notice a wish to be somebody who is helpful to others and who would not carelessly or purposely cause harm to them? Can you notice a wish to be helpful to yourself, and to not carelessly or purposely harm yourself?

Notice how good it feels to be centered in this compassionate-self, just noticing what it would be like if you could be like this—even if it feels difficult. See if you can focus on your commitment to try to be this way. Hold this image in your mind for a few moments on your own. (Pause 45 seconds)

Now imagine what it would be like to move around and interact with the world as your compassionate-self. What would it be like to sit or stand? What voice tones or facial expressions do you notice? See if you can imagine what it's like to be this compassionate-self interacting with the world around you. (Pause 45 seconds)

Now see if you can create an image of yourself at your compassionate best standing in front of you. How would you be dressed? What is your facial expression? What is your posture like? What is this image of you thinking? (Pause 45 seconds)

Now see if you can step into that image of yourself and bring to mind someone that you care deeply about. Try to focus on that person in your mind and notice what wishes you have for them. It might be something like, "I wish for you to be free from suffering" or "I wish for you to have the courage and support that you need to face it." It may just be a sense of wishing them well. Notice this feeling for a moment on your own. (Pause 45 seconds)

Now take a moment to think of an acquaintance or someone you've only briefly crossed paths with. Try to focus on this person for a moment. See if you can feel compassionate motivations towards them as well. Can you wish them well? Notice what it's like to focus on these compassionate motivations with someone you don't know as well. (Pause 45 seconds)

Module 6: Multiple Selves

Aims

- Introduce group members to the concept of multiple selves (multiple emotions and behavior patterns), with a particular focus on threat-based emotions; particularly angry-self, anxious-self, and sad-self.
- Help clients see how these different patterns of mind affect thoughts, bodily states, action impulses, and memories, and have specific ways of settling.
- Discuss ways in which the compassionate-self can serve as a mediator of sorts for the other parts of our self.
- Explain that the compassionate-self helps build insight and understanding, and integrates these different versions of ourselves.

DOI: 10.4324/9781003202493-7

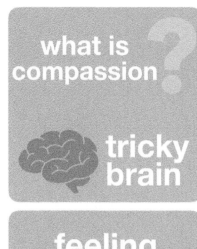

what is compassion ?

tricky brain

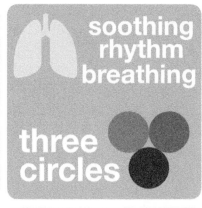

soothing rhythm breathing

three circles

focused attention

mindfulness

feeling safe

other selves

compassionate-self

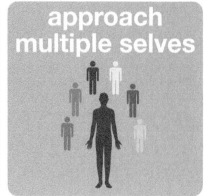

approach multiple selves

Introduction

We've spent time strengthening the compassionate-self, particularly in Module 5. Now, let's take time for a more in-depth look at specific emotions that might cause difficulty. Each emotion will be explored separately. This will help us learn how these different emotions work together and conflicts they can experience. We will then learn how the compassionate-self can help integrate these different emotional mini selves and patterns.

Each of us has different parts and potential patterns that can feel and want different things, and can think in different ways. This can lead to conflict and confusion. We can think of ourselves as having multiple selves. To help us to work with different emotions that can arise at the same time, we're going to use an example of an argument you had with somebody you care about. Ideally this would be a mild argument, just enough to give you an indication of how different feelings and emotions can arise within us. As you go through this exercise, you may find it helpful to use Handout 6.1. Take a moment just bringing to mind an argument with someone you care about. Which emotion usually comes first? Which emotions follow? Which emotions do you prefer, and which would you rather avoid? As this exercise shows, we have many different emotions that we can experience at the same time. Each emotion has its own desire and motivation. For example, often threat emotions are based in some kind of self-protection.

This exercise underlines the idea of **multiplicity**; the idea that we can experience many emotions and motivations at once. Like when peeling an onion with many layers, any experience we have can have layers of emotions and urges. To more thoroughly explore our multiplicity, let's try to slow everything down and look at our various mental states in a bit more detail. Doing this allows us to learn about how to work with them. We have many different types of emotions, but in this module, we're going to look at the three major threat-based emotions, then talk about how our compassionate-self can help us with them. The first is **anger**. Anger is linked to a sense of having been wronged or attacked. Next is **anxiety**. Anxiety is linked to threat and being vulnerable. Finally, there is **sadness,** which is linked to loss. We call these the "big three" because these are the ones that are usually involved the most in our mental health difficulties. Using handout 6.2, we're going to look at how these threat and defensive emotions work against and for you. You'll also see a compassionate-self box on the worksheet. We're going to spend some time talking about ways to involve compassionate-self with these big three emotions.

To help us examine these different threat-based patterns, bring to mind again the mild argument we talked about earlier. The idea is to simply get a sense of how different patterns arise in us and how they work.

Let's start with angry-self because that emotion is often more easily activated. So, just bring that argument to mind, and allow your mind to go over what was said, how it was said, and what you were feeling, thinking, and wanting to do and say. Remember not to get into your anger too deeply at this point. Now let's see if we can explore the different aspects of anger by going through the questions below, which correspond with Handout 6.2. We will lastly consider how we settle, or cope, with emotional overlap or emotions in general. To settle is to limit the effects of an emotion by looking at it through our compassionate eyes.

Table 6.1 Understanding the Self-Critic

Motive	What has triggered your anger? What does angry-self want? What would be a good outcome for anger? What is the function and purpose of your anger? What harmful thing is anger worried about and therefore motivated to try to prevent?
Thoughts	What does angry-self actually think? What are the thoughts that are going through your angry-self's mind? What do you notice arises in your mind when anger comes along?
Body State	What happens in your body when the angry-self and pattern turns up? Where is your feeling in your body? What is your facial expression like? Could you make that expression now? What is your voice tone like? Can you imagine that now? Where in your body does anger go for you? What is your angry body posture? Can you notice how your arms feel right now? What about your hands? If your anger was to build, where would it go in your body?
Actions	What does the angry-self want to do? If anger was in complete control and didn't really care about the consequences, what would it do? What action has come from anger in the past?
Memories	What does the angry-self remember when reflecting on conflicts with others? What memories come to the angry-self? What are the memories that you associate with feeling angry that are particularly powerful or important for you? How far do they go back in time?
Settle	How does your angry-self cope with anger? How does the angry-self settle?

Anger thinks in a particular way, takes over the body in a particular way, has a limited number of action patterns, and comes with memories that go way back. We may try do all kinds of things to try to help it to settle. This is also true of anxiety and sadness.

Now let's take a minute to relax. Take a slightly deeper breath or two and imagine yourselves just letting go of the angry-self/pattern for now. Sometimes it is helpful to say something along the lines of, "Thank you angry-self for coming and explaining your point of view. This has been very helpful." You may find it helpful to go through the exercise once more asking the same questions, but this time for the anxious-self and the sad-self.

Now that we have seen the different aspects, parts, and patterns of ourselves, let's see how they relate to each other.

- What do you think angry-self thinks about anxious-self and sad-self?
- What do you think anxious-self thinks about angry-self and sad-self?
- What do you think sad-self feels about anxious-self and angry-self?

Compassion is important because it enables integration of these different selves. The compassionate-self allows you to see the function of each emotion. **Compassion is rooted in motivation rather than emotion**—so you are shifting out of the threat and harm, avoidance, and protection system (red circle dominated) into the caring motivation system with compassion. The focus of compassion becomes how we form an intention and bring our commitment and wisdom to deal with these various emotions that at times are in conflict. To help you explore how compassion integrates the multiple selves, you may find it useful to listen to "Compassionate-Self for Emotional Growth Regulation and Integration," located at the end of this module. Then go through the table above one more time, this time asking questions as the compassionate-self.

To end, let's imagine how the compassionate mind and self think about the other selves. You may find it helpful to go through Handout 6.3 to explore how the compassionate-self thinks about emotions. First, looking through the eyes and mind of your compassionate-self, what do you make of angry-self? How might you try to help angry-self? As the compassionate-self, what are your thoughts about angry-self?

Let angry-self go and bring to mind anxious-self. Looking through the eyes and mind of your compassionate-self, what do you make of anxious-self? What are you thinking and feeling towards anxious-self? How might you try to help anxious-self?

Now we come to sad-self. Looking through the eyes and mind of your compassionate-self, what do you make of sad-self? What are you thinking and feeling towards sad-self? How might you try to help sad-self? The compassionate-self often acts like a parent in the sense that it does not fight with these other parts of the self, but rather accepts them. In addition, it can understand the thoughts and wishes of these different parts without invalidating them. As the self that values the different selves and integrates them, compassionate-self is key.

To end, "Compassionate-Self Integration of Multiple Selves" is provided. Alternatively, your group leader may have chosen to do the meditation "Cultivating Compassion," which is provided as well.

Discovering Our Innate Multiplicity

Think about a difficult situation, but nothing too distressing. Try to write all of the possible emotions that arise regarding the situation.

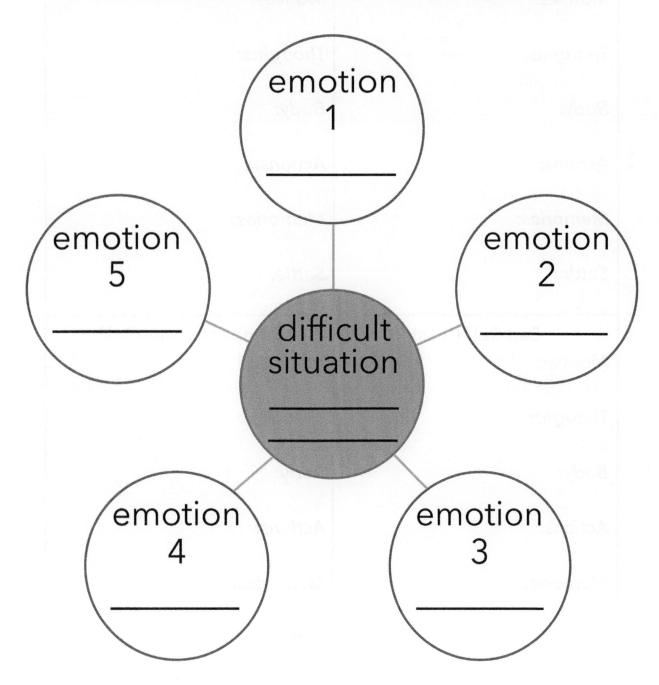

Exploring Multiple Selves in Detail

Angry-Self (offense)	**Anxious-Self (danger)**
Motives:	*Motives:*
Thoughts:	*Thoughts:*
Body:	*Body:*
Actions:	*Actions:*
Memories:	*Memories:*
Settle:	*Settle:*
Sad-Self (loss)	**Compassionate-Self**
Motives:	*Motives:*
Thoughts:	*Thoughts:*
Body:	*Body:*
Actions:	*Actions:*
Memories:	*Memories:*
Settle:	*Settle:*

Compassionate Beliefs about Emotions

Common Beliefs about Emotions	Compassionate Self's Beliefs about Emotions
1. Certain strong emotions are dangerous and easily get out of hand.	1. _____
2. Other people don't feel strong emotions the way I do.	2. _____
3. My emotions are inappropriate.	3. _____
4. If you love somebody, you shouldn't have times when you are angry or even want to leave them.	4. _____
5. If other people love you, they should not be selfish, thoughtless, or have times when they want to leave you.	5. _____
6. You shouldn't have mixed emotions because you should know your mind.	6. _____
7. If people knew what I feel, they would not like me.	7. _____
8. I don't like me because of my feelings.	8. _____
9. I just want to get rid of these feelings.	9. _____
10. _____	10. _____

Module 6 Review

Core Content Themes

- Multiple selves
    - Angry-self, anxious-self, sad-self
    - The different selves have different motives, thoughts, body states, etc.
    - Integration of the "multiple selves" through the compassionate-self

Practice Activities

- Compassionate integration of multiple selves

- Alternate: Cultivating compassion

Compassionate-Self Integration of Multiple Selves

(Note: A digital copy may be provided by your group leader.)

So, we have seen that we have different emotions that pop up when we are engaged in conflict or other life difficulties. These are usually threat emotions, and they can be quite intense. Threat emotions can pull us in a number of different directions. Compassion can help us make space and understand these emotions. Often, we don't want any one of the threat emotions to run the show because, while they all have potential benefits, they also have significant drawbacks. So, we need to tune in to find a part of ourselves that has the courage and the wisdom to act in a way that we want. Using just the angry-self, or just the anxious-self, or just the sad-self may not be the wisest or most helpful approach in managing conflict with, say, someone you care about.

So, you can probably guess which part of ourselves we are going to try to access and see how this part of our self thinks and wants to act.

First, we need to activate our compassionate-self. Always remember that if you stimulate the physiological systems for compassion, it will make it much easier for you to access this part of your mind. (Pause)

Sit with your shoulders back, spine straight, and with an open chest. Remember your friendly facial expression and friendly inner voice tone as we do this exercise.

You may like to close your eyes if you feel comfortable during this next exercise.

Now just bring your attention to your breathing. Connect with your soothing rhythm breathing.

Breathing in 2, 3, 4, 5, and out 2, 3, 4, 5; in 2, 3, 4, 5, and out 2, 3, 4, 5. (Count about a second apart.)

Notice the sensation of mind slowing down, body slowing down. Become more grounded and stable in the body.

Continue to remember your friendly facial expression and friendly voice tone.

Now, it is important to recognize that our compassionate-self is one aspect or one pattern within us. Sometimes this pattern gets pushed aside by these other threat focused parts of us that want to run the show; emotions like anger, or the anxious-self, or the sad-self. These are patterns that are created within us, in our bodies and brains.

So, remember your wisdom that we just all happen to find ourselves here as a part of the flow of life, with our tricky brains. None of us chose to be here. We didn't choose the genes we inherited from our parents. We didn't design our brains to give rise to all kinds of emotions from our threat system, like anger and anxiety, that can also bring about great sadness. Nor did we choose the environments we grew up in, that shaped us for good and perhaps not so good. Therefore, so much has happened that is not our fault. But it is our responsibility to try as best we can to cultivate the help within us. And this is what compassion does. Compassion is wise. Compassion is not weak.

Compassionate wisdom comes from our posture, from our breathing, and from grounding. These all contribute to our strength, authority, and stability. With strength and authority we become stable like a mountain.

Because of our wisdom, we know that we are all caught up in the cycle of life. Because of our courage, we engage with suffering as a part of the flow of life. And because of our commitment, we try to be as helpful, supportive, and kind as we can be when we encounter suffering, whether it be in ourselves or others.

The compassionate-self allows us to pause, recognize that these other patterns are within us, and that they can be triggered at any time. Our compassionate wisdom informs us that these different selves, like angry-self or anxious-self, are coming from our brain that we did not design. Compassionate wisdom tells us that they are coming from our threat system which, while not perfectly skilled, is aimed to protect us. Our compassionate-self can see and recognize this. So, by slowing down, connecting with the breath, and grounding the body, we can reconnect with the compassionate qualities of strength, wisdom, and commitment.

Slowly come back into the room.

Cultivating Compassion

(Note: A digital copy may be provided by your group leader.)

Let's consciously re-visit our intention to develop our compassionate mind and pattern. We start by closing our eyes, or looking down, and feeling how we are sitting in our chair right now.

Settle into your compassion posture with your back straight and shoulders in line with your hips while opening your diaphragm. Now, slow your breathing, and with each slower and deeper breath say, slowly and with a friendly tone, "mind slowing down" and then "body slowing down" on each alternate out breath. Gradually get that sense of grounding, with a sense of stilling or slowing, but also with an alert mind. Notice yourself becoming more grounded. (Allow time for this to settle in, maybe a minute or more.)

Now, start tuning in to your inner compassionate mind and pattern. We bring to mind, attend to, and remember the wisdom that you have been developing in the group so far: We all just find ourselves here with a very tricky brain and certain life experiences that have shaped how our minds and bodies work. Our brain and life experiences have shaped the version of ourselves that we are. And we have a mind that can learn how to change and make choices. So, we are developing the strength and commitment to help ourselves and others address and deal with life and inner difficulties.

Briefly acknowledge yourself for simply being here; with all your doubts, all your resistances, and all your difficulties, but also with the courage and the willingness to go on and to do this path of learning; whatever your current situation is. Acknowledge yourself for giving yourself the opportunity to experience this new learning, for having the courage to stretch your boundaries, even if it's difficult and tricky, and maybe scary. It's scary for everyone.

Acknowledge yourself for being here exactly as you are. Do this in the form of a wish, something like: May I accept myself in this moment of learning exactly as I am; may I give myself all the support and all the kindness I need in this moment; may I accept with compassion all my difficulties; may I accept myself with all my doubts; and may I give myself all the compassion I need in this moment.

Gently ask yourself: "*[Your name], what will you take home from today's session (because you feel it's going to be helpful)?*" And just listen to whatever arises with curiosity.

So, as we are sitting here, we also say in a friendly and committed way:

I am coming here today and over the next weeks in order to:

- Work on ways to be helpful to myself.
- Support others as best I can on their journey.
- Be open to the helpfulness of others.

Okay, now start to let that motivation go. We start coming back slowly into the room, noticing our bodies in the chair, feet on the ground, and when you are ready, you can open your eyes.

Module 7: Self-Criticism

Aims

- Discuss the concept of self-monitoring and how its function is to help us detect danger and perform at our best; it can also result in, however, a disappointment gap when we notice differences between our ideal-self and our actual-self.
- Deepen understanding of the self-critic.
- Explore compassion as an alternative to self-criticism.
- Explore the self-critic through using the compassionate-self.

DOI: 10.4324/9781003202493-8

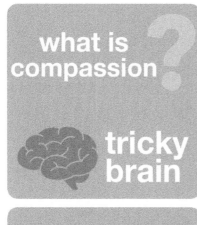
what is compassion
tricky brain

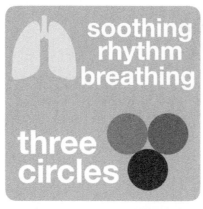
soothing rhythm breathing
three circles

focused attention
mindfulness

feeling safe

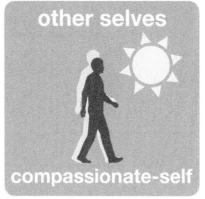
other selves
compassionate-self

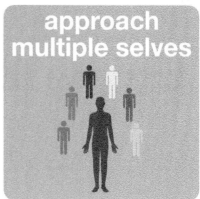
approach multiple selves

encounter the critical-self
and fears

Introduction

This module focuses on self-criticism. We will be examining what self-criticism is, what it can do to us, and how we can use the compassionate mind to work with disappointments and set-backs that often involve a great deal of self-criticism. In compassion focused therapy, criticism takes on three forms: helpful correction, self-attack, and self-hate. The following builds on these three functions.

First, let's think about how and why we monitor ourselves. Let's start with an analogy. Why do we have smoke alarms? Smoke alarms detect smoke and then sound an alarm. Their job is to monitor the air to keep us safe. Similarly, your brain monitors you and your body in very complex ways. Even while you're walking, there is a part of you monitoring your balance so that you don't fall over. If you go for an interview or are meeting somebody new, then part of you will be automatically monitoring how you are doing and how well you are interacting. We constantly monitor what's happening inside of us and around us. This self-monitoring process is vital for self-regulation and social adaptation. Monitoring can be helpful in a correcting way, or it can be harmful when it becomes attacking.

While self-monitoring is important and useful, it can also lead to hurtful self-criticism. In self-monitoring, we compare our thoughts, behaviors, and emotions to some internal standard or ideal. A mismatch between the ideal-self (who we want to be) and actual-self (who we actually are) generates disappointment and sets in motion self-correcting mechanisms. The way we criticize ourselves affects our brain patterns and our bodies.

Ironically, many of us have developed a habit of creating safety for ourselves by being self-critical. We want to protect ourselves from danger or some sort of negative outcome in life. Let's take a closer look at your self-critical voice and its role and function for you. We will do this by exploring how and why we criticize ourselves, seeing whether it is useful or not, and then seeing if switching to a more compassionate way of self-correcting or dealing with setbacks, failures, and disappointments would help us.

Imagine, we could take away your self-criticism so that you'd never get angry with yourself in the future. What would be your greatest fears? What would you worry about if you couldn't do this to yourself anymore? Some typical fears of losing the self-critic include becoming lazy, not learning from mistakes, and not seeing flaws. To explore the inner-critic, please try the experiential exercise "Understanding the Self-Critic" provided near the end of this module. Once completing the exercise, you may find it helpful to fill out Handout 7.1.

Even though we often think that our critical voice is there to help us, actually when we look more deeply, we can see it just makes us feel worse and undermines our confidence. The critical piece of self can be vicious. When this critic really gets going, it makes us depressed and anxious. It also makes us less motivated and enthusiastic to try working towards our goals. It is actually undermining, not inspiring. So, does your critic really have your best interests at heart? Is it wise and does it know how to help you, encourage you, and support you? Is it helping you to achieve your goals—especially when times are hard? Does it offer clear insight for guidance?

The intent of the critical piece of self are usually very useful goals (not to be lazy or arrogant, etc.). However, the self-critic's method of using fear and disappointment of not reaching goals, having a setback, or making a mistake triggers the threat system that can launch attacks, or avoidance. So, we are likely to be more successful by bringing other parts of ourselves into our awareness to encourage and support us than we are to engage in the critical piece that tends to operate by fear, avoidance, and attacking. The compassionate-self is the piece that will encourage and support our efforts!

When we suffer a setback, disappointment, or make a mistake, it is important that we learn ways to deal compassionately with ourselves, without treating the critical attacks as facts about who we are. One of the secrets to success or a happy life is the ability to fail compassionately—it really is the ability to be disappointed, imperfect, or fall short of our ideals without launching attacks on our self. We want to improve, of course, but the vehicle for this improvement is not self-attacking, it is a compassionate self. So, one of the key compassion-based themes of this group says **the secret to success is the ability to fail compassionately**.

This applies to many things in life. For example, if you're learning to drive a car, the first thing is to know how to apply the brakes; if you're learning to swim or canoe, the first thing is to learn how to cope with going under the water; if you're doing judo, the first thing is to learn how to fall. Once we know how to deal compassionately with things that go wrong, we're not frightened of them. It is then that we're free to develop confidence and strengthen our skills. But if we are always monitoring ourselves and are frightened about making mistakes, then we will constantly be putting ourselves down, which makes life more difficult.

Let's close with an analogy. Imagine you have a child you love and you have a choice of two schools. As you walk through the gates to one of the schools, you see a group of teachers that look a lot like your self-critics. They say that they will ensure your child learns because if your child makes mistakes, they will be critical and harsh; they will ensure strong discipline and the fear of authority though punishment. You thank them very much and then you walk to the other school, which is a school filled with compassionate education. At this school, the teachers say they want to help your child feel safe and encourage your child to learn and be enthusiastic about their abilities. When your child makes mistakes, the teachers will support them so that they will learn from mistakes; they will encourage your child to be open, seek help, and be keen to learn how to be better. Your child will feel joy in trying to be the best they can. These compassionate teachers want your child to explore their abilities and talents and see where it takes them rather than be frightened to try. Just as you would want your child to go to the compassionate school, you should also strive to treat yourself with compassion rather than self-criticism. You may find it helpful to fill out Handout 7.2—note how different your self-critic and compassionate-self are. Then to end, the meditation "Compassion Takes the Lead" is provided at the conclusion of this module.

Functional Analysis—Self-Criticism

Greatest fears:

Looks like:	Says to me:	Feels about me:	Does to me:

What I am now thinking and feeling about myself:

Functional Analysis—Self-Criticism

Worked Example

Greatest fears:

Become arrogant; hurt other people; go wild; never get anything done; embarrass myself; be lazy; become a bum; not see where I'm going wrong; be left behind; criticized by others; have no friends.

Looks like:	Says to me:	Feels about me:	Does to me:
Angry self; monster with big mouth and sharp teeth, a greenish slimy thing, black eyes, a big shadow; pointing finger; angry mother; bullying teacher.	You're pathetic; you always are a disappointment; you are a screw up; you aren't good; you're a coward; you're disgusting; if people really knew about you, they wouldn't like you.	Anger; contempt; disappointment; disgust; shame; rejection.	Shut me up; kick me; shake me to wake up; shout; give up on me.

What I am now thinking and feeling about myself:

Sadness; loneliness; anger; tiredness; exhausted; betrayed; depressed; good riddance to the critic.

Functional Analysis—Compassionate-Self

Greatest wishes for me:			

Looks like:	Says to me:	Feels about me:	Does to/for me:

What I am now thinking and feeling about myself:

Functional Analysis—Compassionate-Self

Worked Example

Greatest wishes for me:

Be less egotistical; be true to myself; feel safe; be kind to myself and others; live a valued life; be humble; be helpful; have effort and intention; have courage; keep going if it gets tough.

Looks like:	Says to me:	Feels about me:	Does to/for me:
Mother Earth; butterfly; angel; sunflower; sun; gigantic teddy bear; kind grandmother.	Life is tricky; it's not your fault; let's see what we can do; it is okay; you are okay; this is disappointing but we can try again; you have a good heart.	Unconditional love; care; acceptance; connected; committed; trusting.	Be a support; just be there; hold my hand; act like a friend.

What I am now thinking and feeling about myself:

Light; hopeful; soothed; not judged; energized; accepted.

Tip Sheet on Self-Criticism

1

What do you hope to achieve by listening to your critic?

- Is it helping you?
- What are your greatest fears if your critic was taken away?

2

How would your compassionate-self treat you?

- How does your compassionate-self sound, look, and feel?
- What does it say to you?

3

How do you feel now?

- Is it working?
- What do you feel like doing now?

Module 7 Review

Core Content Themes

- The self-critic
  - Self-monitoring helpful, but can be hurtful
  - Fears associated with letting go of the self-critic
  - Compassionate-self needed instead of the self-critic

- "The secret to success is the ability to fail compassionately"

Practice Activities

- Compassion takes the lead

- Understanding the self-critic

Understanding the Self-Critic

As we do this exercise, go at your own pace and try to remain curious. Don't push yourself too hard, and remember that we're all in this together, trying to figure this out.

Feel free to close your eyes or to look gently down at the ground. Pay attention to your posture, where your shoulders are back, and you feel relaxed but still alert. Now start to slow your breathing just a bit, trying to gradually get into the rhythm of our soothing rhythm breathing exercises. Just slowing your breathing down for a moment to a comfortable, slow rhythm. (Pause)

When you are ready, bring a small thing to mind that you are critical of yourself about—nothing too major to begin with, but just a typical situation that results in you being self-critical or feeling frustrated, annoyed, or disappointed in yourself. See if you can really step into a memory when you were really feeling it, or if you're feeling it now, see if you can really stay with the feeling and notice what it's like. Keep in mind that the idea is not to overwhelm yourself, but to bring up just enough for you to work with. (Pause)

Now that you are in touch with something that you feel self-critical about, imagine you can see this critical part of you, as if it's outside of you, looking back at you. Imagine you can take it out of your head and look at it—see what form it takes. What sort of shape does it have? What colors do you associate with it? You might not see anything clearly, but just try to get a sense of it. Is it dark or light? Does it have a texture? Does it have a form? Just see what kind of sense you get. (Pause about 15–20 seconds.)

As you're looking at it, what is your critic saying to you? What words does it use? What does it think about you? (Pause about 15–20 seconds.)

Now see if you can notice its voice tone or sense of posture. What emotional voice tones does it have? What emotions is it directing at you? How does it feel about you? (Pause about 15–20 seconds.)

What would it like to do to you? See if you can get a sense for what it would like to do. (Pause about 15–20 seconds.)

And what does it want from you? What do you think it wants you to do? (Pause about 15–20 seconds.)

Now allow that image to fade and allow yourself to come back into the room. Notice your breathing again. Bring your attention to the sounds in the room. And when you feel ready, open your eyes.

Compassion Takes the Lead

(Note: A digital copy will be provided by your group leader.)

Let's see if we can take another look at your self-critic and approach it with some compassion.

Go ahead and close your eyes if that's comfortable or look gently down at the floor. Check your posture, noticing your feet flat on the floor, your back in an upright position, slowing your breathing for just a minute. (Pause)

Let's work with that part of ourselves that monitors in a critical way. See if the compassionate part and pattern within you can help it. First, we are giving space to engage our compassionate-self. Slowing the breathing a little, centering our awareness in the body, feeling grounded. Notice that we have our courage and wisdom and commitment to do this work.

Now imagine your critical self in front of you, being critical. You are watching it. Hold to your compassionate position, be your compassionate-self. Now as you are observing the critical piece being critical, see if you can look behind the critic and see what's driving it. Can you see any fears? Rejection? Inferiority? Not being wanted? Consider the pains that brought that fear to life – disappointments or what people may have said? Why is this self-criticism so harsh? Could it be sadness? Loss? What's behind this harsh attitude? Imagine your compassionate-self is curious about the needs and fears of this self-critical part of you.

Holding our compassionate position, we now offer a compassionate wish that "Whatever is causing this desire to be critical of me – to say or feel those things towards me – may this cease and may I find peace from them."

What compassionate message would you like to leave your critical self with? As your compassionate-self, ask yourself these questions: What would you like to hear and to know? What would you need to feel peace?

You might offer messages to your critic such as:

- I see you are frustrated and tired. However, the way you are trying to motivate me is not working. You can rest. I'm doing this job, I'm taking the lead. Thank you for trying.
- I know you are scared or angry, but you can feel safe now. I'm leading the change; everything will be smoother for all of us.
- May you feel safe and at peace.

Slowly bring your attention back to the room as you are ready. Noticing sounds, noticing your body. Opening your eyes.

Module 8: Shame and Guilt

Aims

- Define and discuss shame.
- Explore the experience of shame, including feelings, thoughts, and motivations.
- Distinguish between guilt and shame.
- Practice bringing compassion to shame and trying to shift it towards something more like guilt.

DOI: 10.4324/9781003202493-9

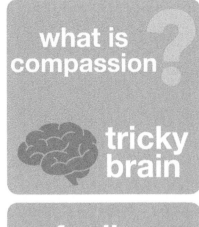

what is compassion ?

tricky brain

soothing rhythm breathing

three circles

focused attention

mindfulness

feeling safe

other selves

compassionate-self

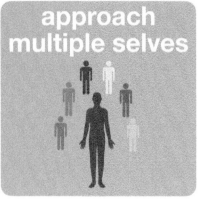

approach multiple selves

encounter the critical-self

and fears

healing from shame

it's not your fault

Introduction

In the last module, we looked at the issue of self-criticism. This module will explore another set of emotions that can undermine us or damage relationships, leaving us feeling anxious and depressed. We call these shame-based emotions. In this module, we will see how, just like with self-criticism, the compassionate-self can help us deal with shame and shame-based self-criticism.

Before looking at our shame-based emotions, let's explore how our brains have evolved. When animals compete with each other for resources, what happens if one feels weaker and vulnerable to the other? Typically, the weaker animal will be submissive, and the stronger animal will be dominant. Like animals, some people tend to mostly be anxious and submissive, whereas others are very quick to become aggressive. Interestingly, the more powerful you feel, the more likely you go for the latter. For example, bosses are more likely to respond to criticism from subordinates with aggression than subordinates who are criticized by bosses. If bosses criticize subordinates, the subordinates are more likely to close down, apologize, appease, or even try to hide. Power dynamics are quite important in how we deal with social threats.

Knowing that some of what we experience when we face social threats are a result of the way our brains are built, we can begin to explore different aspects of how we experience social threats. These are called **self-conscious** or **social emotions**, and they are linked to our feelings about ourselves. For example, if we are frightened of being rejected because people don't like us, then this is called a self-conscious emotion. Self-conscious emotions can be positive as well as negative. For example, on the positive side, pride is linked to the feeling that other people admire or like you in some way. The family of shame emotions are on the negative side and are related to things we feel about ourselves if we think other people do not approve of us.

Shame is an important self-conscious emotion to understand. Typically, when we feel shame, we feel it in a global sense of ourselves. For example, if we feel ashamed about our appearance, we typically think we are ugly or unattractive. There are two aspects to shame that we call internal and external. With **external shame**, our attention and our focus go outwards towards what *others* think and feel about *us*. With **internal shame**, our attention and our focus go inwards towards what *we* think and feel about *ourselves*. This connects to our last module, where we looked at self-criticism and how we can put ourselves down. It is important for us to understand that underneath all of that self-criticism is actually the fear of external shame, which is the fear of disapproval, social rejection, and isolation. Typically, internal and external shame go together, but not always. For example, we can be very sensitive to external shame without necessarily feeling bad about ourselves. Equally, we can feel bad about ourselves, while believing that other people feel good about us. To explore the issue of shame more in depth, *imagine revealing something that you feel ashamed of. Then fill out Handout 8.1.* This exercise is meant to help you notice that there is no particular emotion associated with shame. Different people will have different emotions. Some will talk about anxiety and fear, while others might talk about feeling irritated and put on the spot. Others might talk in terms of feeling closed down. However, most people tend to 1) believe that other people will think negatively about them, and 2) distance themselves from people as a result of these fears.

Another self-conscious emotion is **guilt**, which is perhaps one of the most poorly understood emotions. It is often confused with shame, though shame and guilt are actually quite different. Guilt is the regret we feel when we have caused harm, and it evolved from the caring system. When mammals evolved caring behavior, they also had to evolve ways of detecting and avoiding harm to those they cared for. It turns out guilt is linked to this harm avoidance, and it inspires us to try to repair harm if we cause it. With guilt, we are not that bothered about whether people look down on us or like us. We are not concerned about defending ourselves with appeasing, hiding, or fighting. Actually, the emotion of guilt is one of sadness with remorse, not anxiety or anger. In guilt, we are not focusing on ourselves as individuals, but on our specific behaviors or harmful things we have done and the desire to improve.

Note how shame is different from guilt. Shame tends to be much more self-focused. If we have been harmful and try to repair that harm out of shame, then basically we try to help ourselves feel better. We want the other person to forgive us and like us again. In contrast, guilt is behavior focused. Guilt requires empathy, whereas shame does not. As an example, imagine that two people (we'll call them Tom and Harry) both have cheated on their significant others, and that their cheating is then discovered. Tom feels shame because he automatically thinks, "Oh, people will not like me now, and my wife will be angry and not love me!" He is focusing on what the world thinks about him. He might also feel bad about himself (e.g., "I'm a bad person to have done this."). All of his focus is on himself. This is called shame.

Harry, on the other hand, does not focus on himself but on the harm that he has done, with a great sense of remorse and sorrow for the upset he has caused. His genuine wish is to make amends, or support the person he has hurt. His attention is not on himself, but on the harm he has done. This is called guilt. Now, in fact, guilt is very important for us because when we are open to guilt, we are open to recognizing how we can hurt people, often unintentionally. This allows us to take responsibility and turn our focus to putting things right, if we can. Remember, in compassion focused therapy, our intention is always to try to address suffering and certainly not cause it.

We have looked at many different feelings related to external shame, internal shame, and guilt. These can seem a little tricky to understand, so using Handout 8.2, let's think of some examples to help us.

In this group, we are aiming to heal shame and to shift from shame to guilt. Courage is the core process of healing shame. The intensity of shame diminishes when we begin to accept our vulnerabilities as human beings and reach out to reconnect to others. To close, the exercise "Shifting from Shame to Guilt" is provided, as well as the meditation "Developing a Compassionate Intention."

Exploring Shame

What feelings arose for me when I thought I might have to reveal something shameful?

What do I typically think about how other people would react and treat me as a result?	**In the moment, how do I typically react when I feel shame?**	**How do I typically cope when I feel shame?**

How has shame influenced my life?

Shame vs. Guilt

For each situation below, consider these questions and think about shame and guilt-based responses to them.

- What would a shame response be like?
- What would a guilt response be like?
- Which of those would you prefer and would be most helpful?
- How would your compassionate-self help you?

Imagine that you lose your temper with a child, and you shout at them.

Imagine that you forget your friend's birthday, and they call you up to remind you.

Imagine that because life has become difficult you turn to drugs, and that has negative consequences.

Think of a personal situation when you caused harm to someone else.

Module 8 Review

Core Content Themes

- Self-conscious emotions: shame and guilt
  - Definitions of shame and guilt
  - Shifting from shame to guilt

Practice Activities

- Developing a compassionate intention

- Shifting from shame to guilt

Shifting from Shame to Guilt

Let's take a moment to see if we can shift from a global sense of shame to a more specific sense of guilt around something. Start by allowing yourself to close your eyes or look gently at the floor and notice what it's like to be breathing right now, in and out. Try to remember that each new breath is a new moment, different from the last. Just sit with your breathing for a moment. (Pause)

Now see if you can bring to mind a time when you felt ashamed about something you did—don't make it the most major thing in your life, but just something that gave you a bit of a sense of shame. Notice the emotions that come. Notice if they are global rather than specific, if they are focused on you rather than others, or if they make you want to hide rather than repair. If so, these are feelings of shame.

Let's see if we can shift those feelings, first by bringing a sense of compassion to this shame. Can you think about how your ideal compassionate other might interact with you around this shame—what might they think about you? What might they say? How would they feel about you? Or you may want to see if you can activate a sense of self-compassion around this shame, understanding the tricky brain and how difficult it is to be human, and recognizing the pain you're experiencing. See if you can find a way to bring some compassion to this sense of shame. (Pause for at least one minute.)

And now, see if you can try to shift from shame to guilt—from global to specific—from a sense of wanting to hide to a sense of wanting to repair—from worrying mostly about yourself to also considering others. This may be a difficult shift to make, and if you're having difficulty, remember that that is normal. Just try to stay with an intention to shift from shame to guilt, or a wish to do so. Try to stay with this intention for a few moments on your own. (Pause for at least one minute.)

And now, when you feel ready, begin to let go of that intention, and notice what it's like to be in this room, sitting in your chair, breathing. And when you feel ready, open your eyes.

Developing a Compassionate Intention

(Note: A digital copy will be provided by your group leader.)

Now that we have developed some practices for working with shame, we can take a moment to bring our module to a close for today. Let's consciously re-visit our intention to develop our compassionate mind and pattern. Start by closing your eyes or looking down. Take a moment and just notice the sensations of sitting in your chair right now. (Pause 15 seconds.)

Settle into your compassion posture with your back straight and shoulders in line with your hips, while opening your diaphragm. Now slow your breathing, and with each slower and deeper breath say, slowly and with a friendly tone, "mind slowing down" and then "body slowing down" alternatively. Gradually get that sense of grounding with a sense of stilling/slowing, but also with an alert mind. Notice yourself becoming more grounded. (Allow time for this to settle in—maybe a minute or more.)

Now start tuning in to your inner compassionate mind and pattern. Bring to mind, attend to, and remember the wisdom that you have been developing in the course so far. We all just find ourselves here with a very tricky brain and certain life experiences that have shaped how our minds and bodies work and the version of ourselves that we are. However, we also have a mind that can learn how to change and make choices. Therefore, we are developing the strength and commitment to help ourselves and others to address and deal with life and inner difficulties.

Briefly acknowledge yourself for simply being here; with all your doubts, all your resistances, and all your difficulties. Also, acknowledge your courage and willingness to go on and engage in this path of learning; whatever the current situation is. Acknowledge yourself for giving yourself the opportunity to experience this new learning, for having the courage to stretch your boundaries, even if it's difficult and tricky, and maybe scary. It's scary for everyone. Acknowledge yourself for being here exactly as you are. Do this in the form of a wish, something like: May I accept myself in this moment of learning exactly as I am. May I give myself all the support and all the kindness I need in this moment. May I accept with compassion all of my difficulties, all of my doubts. May I give myself all the compassion I need in this moment.

Notice how the same air touches everybody in the room and connects you with the group. Sense the presence of the people around you for several breaths. Now, bring to mind that we are all human beings. Like all the billions of human beings outside this room, we all have experiences of shame, discomfort, anger, and anxiety. We all have experiences or fantasies we would not want to share with others. Shame is one of the shared life challenges we can all struggle with and face. We all have vulnerabilities, weaknesses, and flaws. We all make mistakes. We all sometimes struggle with aspects of our personality. We are all part of this flow of life. At the same time, we are here, together, facing this deeply isolating emotion with the strength, wisdom, and commitment of the compassionate-self. Just being here, as we are, is a sign that we are starting to approach this emotion with the willingness to heal.

Experience the connectedness with the group and all other human beings for several breaths.

Okay, now start letting that motivation go. We slowly start coming back into the room, noticing our bodies in the chair and feet on the ground. When you are ready, you can open your eyes.

Module 9: Deepening Compassion for the Self

Aims

- Deepen compassion for the self.
- Use compassionate mind states to address issues.
- Introduce techniques to switch to compassionate-self (deepening breathing, flashcards, compassionate letter writing, compassionate behavioral planning, and compassion at the mirror).

DOI: 10.4324/9781003202493-10

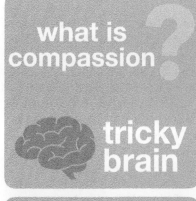

what is compassion ?

tricky brain

soothing rhythm breathing

three circles

focused attention

mindfulness

feeling safe

other selves

compassionate-self

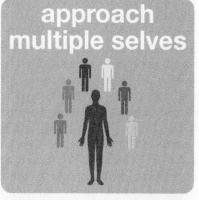

approach multiple selves

encounter the critical-self

and fears

healing from shame

it's not your fault

compassionate letter writing

Introduction

We have now discovered how self-conscious emotions can stem from different motivational systems, and how the compassionate-self can help us deal with shame and shame-based self-criticism. In this module, we will be looking more deeply and working more closely with developing compassion for ourselves.

Like we've been talking about before, we are all made by genes that we didn't choose. We didn't choose two arms and two legs. We didn't choose to be a woman or a man. We didn't choose to be born into this culture at this time. We didn't choose to have the brain that we have with the emotions that it's capable of. The first step in compassion, then, is to see ourselves as a version that we may or may not like and to realize that we are just one version of many possible versions. The second step to compassion for self is to recognize that we all have a motivation for caring and compassion. This compassion can help us organize some of the more tricky and threat-based stuff that gets activated in our minds through no fault of our own.

Remember our definition of compassion. It is that we are sensitive to the suffering of self and others and that we make a commitment to try the best we can to alleviate and prevent such suffering. At its simplest, compassion is the desire to be helpful and not harmful to self and others. Sometimes this can be a lot easier said than done. For a minute, think about the extent over the last few weeks that you have noticed yourself trying to be helpful rather than harmful. Don't worry if sometimes you feel it hasn't gone so well; that's just how it is. Try to bring to mind times over the past few weeks when you were helpful even in small ways. This could be to friends or family or children or strangers. Just try for a moment to switch into that part of yourself that would like to be helpful. How does this feel? Okay, so now let's take that same idea of compassion and try to apply it to ourselves. We may be living in a version of ourselves that has had a lot of trauma or difficulty, or we may be living in a version that tends to be critical and blame ourselves a lot. Let's really try to tap into the version of ourselves that is compassionate toward ourselves and our unique situation. How is this like? Take a minute and look back over the past few weeks and try to bring to mind times when you've tried to be helpful and understanding of yourself rather than neglectful, hurtful, or harmful. You may think about times that you practiced your breathing, times you thought kindly about yourself and your situation, times you were more careful with your self-criticism, etc. How is this to think about?

Compassionate Letter Writing

We are now going to explore practices for deepening our self-compassion. There are a couple of practices we can do today. *Our first exercise will be Handout 9.1: Compassionate Letter Writing.* Before you begin, let's access our compassionate mind. Try to feel that part of you that can be kind and understanding of others; how you would be and act if you were caring for someone you like. Consider your general manner, facial expressions, voice tone, and feelings that come with your caring-self. Think about that part of you as the type of self you would like to be. Think about the qualities you would like your compassionate-self to have. It does not matter if you feel you are like this—but focus on the ideal you would like to be. Spend a few moments really thinking about this and trying to feel in contact with this "kind" part of yourself. Think to yourself about something you feel you would like to gain support or understanding about; it could be a life difficulty or anything you want. A few pointers for you. The letter should not be giving you advice or talk in terms of should, need to's, must's, etc. Rather focus on the following:

1 Indicating an understanding and empathy for your difficulty.
2 Showing genuine support and caring.
3 Focusing on your courage and your strengths.
4 Noticing opportunities for supports or anything helpful.
5 Not offering instructions or should statements that are unhelpful.

Some of you might worry about your spelling, grammar, or something else. These things don't matter for this exercise. You might also notice that starting this letter can be a little tricky, so just start writing anything you want. You can start by writing your name, *"Dear ..."* And you can write in any way you want. There is no right or wrong way to do this...whatever seems right for you is great. As you start writing, you may be aware of all kinds of distractions that will pull you off course, such as being critical, feeling you won't do it right, or that you are being silly. Whatever distraction or resistance comes up, try to remember that all of those thoughts can veer your mind away from the task of being compassionate. When you notice your mind veering, just try to pull it back to the task at hand as best you can. It's okay that your mind does this. Once you feel ready, please complete the exercise.

Compassionate Behavioral Planning

We can also build compassion for the self through compassionate behavioral planning. We've seen that we can take a life difficulty and shift into our compassionate mind states, and try to generate some ideas that would be helpful to us. We are also able to think about those coping ideas from a compassionate-self mindset. While doing this, we can continue to remind ourselves that life can be very difficult without any easy answers, but we are trying to do the best we can. So, let's try to think about building compassionate behavior into our everyday living. Try to generate some ideas about how we could practice certain behaviors during the week that would be examples of compassionate behavior. You may want to give yourself more time to do soft landing practices. Or, you can make a goal to spend time with a friend more frequently. Maybe you need to focus more on things that you do well on. Just think of behaviors that would help you. Let's remind ourselves that when we think and react from a compassionate mindset, even when we don't necessarily feel like doing so, our behaviors can shift as well.

At the end of this module, three other exercises to deepen compassion are provided for you to try: (1) **Compassionate Breathing and Compassionate Light, Mist, or Energy,** (2) **Using a Compassionate Mind to Help Us with a Life Difficulty—Flashcards**, and (3) **Compassion at the Mirror**. Some people will find an exercise very helpful, but not everybody will. So, there are several for you to try so you can see which of these exercises work for you or don't work for you. Following these exercises, a closing meditation is provided.

Compassionate Letter Writing

First Steps

1. **Think** about something that makes you feel shame, insecure, or not good enough.
2. **Notice** how it makes you feel.
3. **Activate** your compassionate-self.

Acknowledge, without judgment, the pain of your suffering self.	*I acknowledge the difficulty of…*
Engage empathetic acceptance and understanding.	*I understand…*
Commit or re-commit to alleviate suffering and desire to look for resources that support and strengthen (care for well-being).	*I want to tell you that…* *To get there, you could…*

<u>The following principles may be useful whenever you write a compassionate letter to yourself:</u>

- Be sensitive to and validate the emotions you experience.
- Convey understanding, acceptance, and caring.
- Validate the reasons you may be struggling with certain things.
- Recognize that human beings are a complex species, and this means we often struggle.
- Recognize that we are all prone to self-criticism, and although your self-critic has your best intentions at heart, listening to it is not the best way to feel better.
- Remain nonjudgmental.
- Reflect on which of the emotion regulation systems would be helpful for you to work on at the moment.
- Remind yourself that you are not on your own. Millions of other people struggle to build their self-confidence.
- Recognize that life can be hard, and sometimes other people can do things that hurt us.
- Rather than avoid difficult situations, allow yourself to be moved by your own experiences.

<u>These could be compassionate wishes:</u>

- I know you and accept you deeply, exactly as you are, in this very moment.
- I'll never abandon you, and I'll be here with you until you feel better and until we find together a way to go through this storm.
- My deepest intention and desire will always be that you can feel good and you can flourish.
- I'll always be here for you. You can always count on me especially when you feel the worst. It's when I really want to be there with you, it's where I want to feel I'm there with you.
- My deepest desire is that you can be compassionate and encouraging with yourself, no matter what.
- My deepest desire is that you really feel how not alone you are in this pain.
- I want to help you find a way to meet your deepest needs, and I also know how difficult this search could be. This is why I'm here with you.
    - Maybe you could….[suggest ways for yourself to meet your emotional needs].
- But overall, I just want to let you know how deeply I care for you and how much I desire to be close to you in all the ups and downs of this life.

Module 9 Review

Core Content Themes

- Deepening compassion for the self
  - Compassionate letter writing and other self-compassion exercises

Practice Activities

- Cultivating compassion
- Compassionate breathing and compassionate light, mist, or energy
- Using a compassionate mind to help us with a life difficulty—flashcards
- Compassion at the mirror

Compassionate Breathing and Compassionate Light, Mist, or Energy

We are now going to do an exercise to deepen our self-compassion. Let's begin by sitting in your chair with your compassionate posture of shoulders back, open diaphragm, and a concave curve in the back. Allow your breath to come down deeper into your diaphragm and find your soothing rhythm breathing rate at around five breaths per minute. Even and regular. (Pause for about a minute.)

Now just focus on the fact that the breath coming into you is also life-sustaining. Without it, you, of course, would die. Imagine you are taking in life-giving breath and try to feel that breath really sustaining you. Feel its life-giving properties move around in your lungs and maybe even flowing around your body to sustain you and to support you. (Pause for about a minute.)

Now imagine that you are surrounded by a compassionate light, mist, or energy. As you breathe in, you are breathing in this compassionate light, mist, or energy and allowing it to move around in your body, bringing compassion to all parts of your body. We now have compassion in our lungs, compassion in our heart, compassion in our stomach, compassion down into the legs. Imagine that as you breathe in the compassionate light, mist, or energy, that it is also going up into your head, filling it with its compassionate, soothing energy. (Pause for about a minute.)

Now we will add a slight motivation. Imagine that this compassionate light, mist, or energy is soothing, but also trying to heal. That is its job and function. Just like water can wash away things in its path, imagine that healing is the function of this light, mist, or energy. It has no other motivation than to heal you, soothe you, and help all the parts of your body, including your mind that may be suffering in various ways. (Pause for about a minute.)

Now imagine your whole body is constituted of this compassionate light, mist, or energy and you have a body of light. It might be a bright light or it may have a color; whatever seems good for you. (Pause for about a minute.)

Sometimes it can be helpful to think of our compassionate-self with this compassionate energy or light in it. When we begin to deepen the compassionate-self, we are deepening our sense of being connected to the world around us; even the air we breathe is fundamental to our existence. We are a part of the flow of life.

Using a Compassionate Mind to Help Us with a Life Difficulty—Flashcards

We're now going to use our compassionate mind to help us with a life difficulty. Please find a piece of paper for you to write some notes on if you want. Bring to mind a life difficulty. Again, nothing too major that would overwhelm. The idea is always to challenge yourself but not to overwhelm yourself. From the position of your compassionate mind, how would you ideally like to deal with this difficulty? We recognize that we often can't make things go away, but we can learn to tolerate and cope with them in different ways that are more helpful. (Pause)

Without blaming or shaming, just focus on trying to be helpful. How understanding are you of this difficulty? Could you be more understanding or more empathetic toward yourself? What would that be like? (Pause)

Now let's use our empathy and understanding. What do you need to know? What would be helpful to you right now to deal with this difficulty? (Pause)

Let's turn this into a flashcard. To do this, we're going to think of three or four really helpful thoughts, ideas, or statements for you to remember, and to say in a compassionate way, at the time you need them. If you're unsure, you can ask others in the group for their ideas too.

Now that you have generated some coping thoughts, ideas, and statements, let's move into the compassionate mindset and really focus on thinking through those coping ideas. Try saying some of these with a compassionate intention and with a kind and gentle voice tone that has a deep wisdom and understanding.

Compassion at the Mirror

We tend to look at ourselves in the mirror only in an "analytical way," trying to spot imperfections or to observe details. Not very often (or maybe ever) do we look at our own face in its "fullness," like we usually observe other people's faces, from an external point of view.

The way we view other people and the way others view us is generally more friendly and compassionate than the way we normally look at ourselves. In a sense, our own view of ourselves can be biased by many experiences, memories, and conditioning—these things can change the way we literally see ourselves.

We will now use a mirror to really "meet" ourselves and to facilitate that empathetic process. Keep in mind that it is very likely that many resistances will arise: we will be distracted by our physical imperfections and our desire to fix them—this is part of the exercise and is to be expected. We might even see things about our face that we don't like very much (red system). Remember that such responses are completely natural. Actually, they are at the core of this practice. Our practice of becoming more compassionate toward ourselves becomes stronger every time we commit to meet our resistances with compassion.

Our goal is to repeatedly return to our compassionate mind. How would our compassionate-self look at our self, especially in a moment of suffering? What kind of gaze would they have on us? Or, how would we look at the face of a friend in a moment of suffering? Would we look at imperfections in their face? The practice helps us move with compassionate intention toward the suffering and painful emotions that our face might express.

Now, take your mirror and, at first, just look at yourself in the way you would normally. Where does your attention go? What are the thoughts that pop up into your mind? Are they critical thoughts?

Now, close your eyes and settle into your compassion posture with your back straight and shoulders in line with your hips, while opening your diaphragm. Now slow your breathing, and with each slower and deeper breath say, slowly and with a friendly tone, "mind slowing down" and then "body slowing down."

Now, bring to mind, attend to, and remember the wisdom that you have been developing so far: that we all just find ourselves here with a very tricky brain and certain life experiences that have shaped how our minds and bodies work. Refocus on the desire to help, to alleviate the suffering that you encounter as best as you can. Refocus on the strength and commitment to help ourselves and others address and deal with life and inner difficulties.

Now, from this position of inner wisdom and strength, and with the only intention to give support, to help and to try to alleviate the suffering that you meet, gently open your eyes. Commit to look at your own face in the mirror from the perspective of your compassionate-self.

What does your compassionate-self notice in that face in the mirror? (Pause 15 seconds.) Does your compassionate-self notice any sign of discomfort or suffering? (Pause 15 seconds.)

The compassionate-self is really interested and able to see what is behind those eyes. What do they see? What are the needs, sometimes unmet needs, that those eyes express? (Pause 15 seconds.)

Now, really connecting with the deep desire to bring relief, say something that could really help that person in the mirror. Connecting with wisdom and strength, what kind of facial expression would your compassionate-self have toward that suffering person? (Pause 15 seconds.)

What kind of smile? (Pause 15 seconds.)

What kind of gaze could express a deep understanding and a desire to help? (Pause 15 seconds.)

Now, if the compassionate-self had to say something to that person in the mirror, something that comes from the heartfelt desire to be of support and of help, and to bring some kind of relief to that suffering person, what would they say? What would be the words that person would really need to hear in this very moment? Whisper it, as best as you can, with the intention to bring help, support, relief, and maybe courage. (Pause 15 seconds.)

Use the compassionate intention as an anchor. Every time your mind wanders away, simply realize that it's normal. Kindly come back to the commitment to meet that face and those eyes in the mirror with a compassionate intention. Indeed, you probably would not stop trying to convey your intent to care for a friend, even if at the beginning they felt reluctant. Actually, the core of this exercise is to kindly and patiently work with that reluctance and to stick with our compassionate intent toward our suffering, especially when we feel embarrassment or think we don't deserve it.

If you feel that the practice is becoming too intense, just close your eyes again and connect to your soothing rhythm breathing. Gently remember that it's natural to feel resistances, that it is not your fault: our brains and our experiences have often made us reluctant and even afraid to experience certain types of emotion. Just welcome this resistance and come back to the intention to meet the suffering that you might notice in your own eyes with compassion. And when you are ready, you can open up your eyes again and tell yourself the compassionate phrases that you have used before, or some other phrases that you might feel are more appropriate now.

Gentle repetition is important to really convey a sense of "I'm really here for you," especially when resistances arise.

Cultivating Compassion

(Note: A digital copy will be provided by your group leader.)

Let's consciously re-visit our intention to develop our compassionate-mind and pattern. We start by closing our eyes or looking down, or closing our eyes, and noticing how we feel siting in our chair right now.

Settle into your compassion posture with your back straight and shoulders in line with your hips, while opening your diaphragm. Now slow your breathing, and with each slower and deeper breath say, slowly and with a friendly tone "mind slowing down" and then "body slowing down." Alternate these phrases on each out breath—gradually get that sense of grounding with a sense of stilling/slowing, but also with an alert mind. Notice yourself becoming more grounded. (Allow time for this to settle in—maybe a minute or more.)

Now, start tuning in to your inner compassionate-mind and pattern. We bring to mind, attend to, and remember the wisdom that you have been developing in the course so far: We all just find ourselves here with a very tricky brain and certain life experiences that have shaped how our minds and bodies work—shaping the version of ourselves that we are. But we have a mind that can learn how to change and make choices, so we are developing the strength and commitment to help ourselves and others address and deal with life and inner difficulties.

Briefly acknowledge yourself for simply being here; with all your doubts, all your resistances, and all your difficulties, but also with the courage and the willingness to go on and to do this path of learning, whatever the current situation is. Acknowledge yourself for giving yourself the opportunity to experience this new learning, for having the courage to stretch your boundaries, even if it's difficult, tricky, and maybe scary. It's scary for everyone. Acknowledge yourself for being here exactly as you are. Do this in the form of a wish. Something like: May I accept myself in this moment of learning exactly as I am; may I give myself all the support and all the kindness I need in this moment; may I accept with compassion all my difficulties, all my doubts; and may I give myself all the compassion I need in this moment.

Gently ask yourself: "[*Your name*], *what do you want to take home from today's session (because you feel it's going to be helpful)?*" And just listen to whatever arises with curiosity.

So, as we are sitting here, we also say in a friendly and committed way:

I am coming here today and over the next weeks in order to:

- Work on ways to be helpful to myself.
- Support others as best I can on their journey.
- Be open to the helpfulness of others.

Okay, now start letting that motivation go. Start coming back slowly into the room, notice your bodies in the chair, feet on the ground, and when you are ready, you can open your eyes.

Module 10: Compassionate Assertiveness

Aims

- Introduce and define compassionate assertiveness (what it is and is not).
- Apply assertiveness to interpersonal conflict.
- Distinguish passive, aggressive, passive-aggressive, and compassionate assertive communication patterns.
- Explore ways to ask for what we need using compassionate assertiveness.
- Demonstrate how assertiveness helps us to connect with others in interpersonal conflict, expressing appreciation, asking for what we need, and responding to criticism.

DOI: 10.4324/9781003202493-11

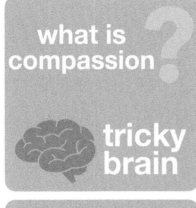

what is compassion ?

tricky brain

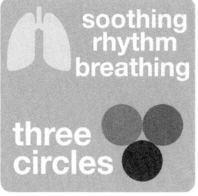

soothing rhythm breathing

three circles

focused attention

mindfulness

feeling safe

other selves

compassionate-self

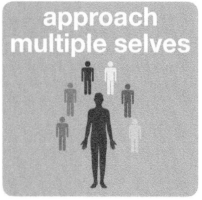

approach multiple selves

encounter the critical-self

and fears

healing from shame

it's not your fault

compassionate letter writing

compassionate assertiveness

Introduction

We have been spending time in group strengthening our compassionate-self. Our compassionate-self can help us to feel grounded and can also help mediate the other parts of ourselves. In this module, we're going to build on these skills by focusing on compassionate assertiveness.

Let's take a look at what compassionate assertiveness is. First of all, it is different than submission and aggression. Sometimes there is a perception that in order to be compassionate, you have to be nice or do what other people say even if it is not a healthy thing for you. Some think that if a person is compassionate, they shouldn't express their own points of view. Compassion is not synonymous with being weak. On the other hand, when people hear the word "assertive," they may think of someone being rude or aggressive. Compassionate assertiveness is not aggression, nor is it about "giving-in" or being "submissive." Compassionate assertiveness is learning to be clear about your own values, wishes, wants, and needs. It helps us to have the strength and authority to say no to others when we need to and decide when we can say yes appropriately. Compassionate assertiveness is giving clear and direct messages while also being open to critical feedback from others without responding defensively. Assertiveness ties into the strength and authority aspect of compassion.

The aim of the assertive-self is to clarify your own personal experience while avoiding inducing fear, guilt, and so forth. An example of a compassionately assertive response to a criticism might look like, "When I hear that, it really hurts me. I get upset because I think you don't care." With a compassionately assertive response, you begin by describing what's happening inside of you ("it really hurts") rather than attacking ("you are a jerk"). Depending on the criticism, you might own your own behavior by saying something like, "I can see my behavior has irritated or upset you. That was not my intention so I'm sorry...." When we are assertive, we pay significant attention to our facial expressions and our voice tones (which can be quite threatening to others when left unchecked). When we are assertive, we show our willingness to listen to the other person and communicate with the intent of understanding what upset them. Listening in this way, we try to come to a compromise that works for both and demonstrate respect for others and ourselves. When we listen in this way, we give the other the space they may need as well. The goal of assertiveness is to take the heat out of the conflict. Because it's the heat, rather than the issue, that often causes the problem. To more thoroughly explore compassionate assertiveness, let's take a look at Handout 10.1 to see some examples.

There's a lot more to assertiveness than simply dealing with conflicts. Assertiveness is linked to a confident desire to be clear about how we feel. Assertiveness is about clearly communicating our desires while being committed to being helpful and supportive of others. Assertive is not being selfish! Being assertive also means that we are prepared for reasonable compromise.

It's important to remember that compassionate assertiveness, like every other skill we've talked about so far, takes time and practice to develop. It takes time to be aware of and practice altering our body posture and voice tone when communicating assertively with others. There may also be some consequences associated with assertiveness. For example, not everyone responds well to assertiveness. We can become worried about others not liking us if we are assertive and express boundaries. We may even begin to feel bad about ourselves if we set boundaries and view ourselves as not being able to do "everything." To practice compassionate assertiveness, think about when others have been critical of you. They may have explicitly stated, "I don't like you," or they may have rolled their eyes. Then, imagining how the different "selves" would respond to those criticisms, fill out Handout 10.2. Then to close, there is a meditation to conclude this module.

Components of Compassionate Assertiveness

ASSERTIVENESS

- is confidence
- is the ability to express dissatisfaction, concerns, and upsets
- is recognizing that our interpretations may be the source of our hurt rather than what was actually said or intended
- allows us to acknowledge and admit our limitations or mistakes without feeling shame
- allows us to initiate an opinion or choice and helps us to be prepared for others to disagree without feeling attacked or shamed
- allows us to take the lead in praising others and acknowledging their helpfulness
- allows us to be open to the helpfulness of others
- is being genuinely empathetic to ourselves and others

Essentially, compassionate assertiveness is trying to understand clearly our own minds and the minds of others.

Exploring Multiple Selves in Detail

Angry-Self (offense)	**Anxious-Self (danger)**
Thoughts:	*Thoughts:*
Body:	*Body:*
Actions:	*Actions:*
Memories:	*Memories:*
Settle:	*Settle:*
Needs (Motives):	*Needs (Motives):*
Sad-Self (loss)	**Compassionate-Self**
Thoughts:	*Thoughts:*
Body:	*Body:*
Actions:	*Actions:*
Memories:	*Memories:*
Settle:	*Needs (Motives):*
Needs (Motives):	

Module 10 Review

Core Content Themes

- **Understanding the definition and components of "compassionate assertiveness"**

Practice Activities

- **Cultivating compassion**

Cultivating Compassion

(Note: A digital copy will be provided by your group leader.)

Let's consciously re-visit our intention to develop our compassionate mind and pattern. We start by closing our eyes or looking down and feeling how we are sitting in our chair right now. Settle into your compassionate posture with your back straight and shoulders in line with your hips, while opening your diaphragm. Now slow your breathing, and with each slower and deeper breath say, slowly and with a friendly tone, "mind slowing down" and then "body slowing down," alternating on each out breath. Gradually, get that sense of grounding; that sense of stilling or slowing but also with an alert mind. Notice yourself becoming more grounded. (Pause for a minute or so.)

Now, start tuning in to your inner compassionate mind and pattern. Bring to mind, attend to, and remember the wisdom that you have been developing in the course so far: We all just find ourselves here with a very tricky brain and certain life experiences that have shaped how our minds and bodies work—shaping the version of ourselves that we have become. But we have a mind that can learn how to change and make choices, so we are developing the strength and commitment to help ourselves and others address and deal with life and inner difficulties.

Briefly acknowledge yourself for simply being here, with all your doubts, all your resistances, and all your difficulties, but also with the courage and the willingness to go on and to do this path of learning, whatever the current situation is. Acknowledge yourself for giving yourself the opportunity to experience this new learning, for having the courage to stretch your boundaries, even if it's difficult and tricky, and maybe scary. It's scary for everyone.

Acknowledge yourself for being here exactly as you are. Do this in the form of a wish, something like: May I accept myself in this moment of learning exactly as I am; may I give myself all the support and all the kindness I need in this moment; may I accept with compassion all my difficulties, all my doubts; and may I give myself all the compassion I need in this moment.

Gently ask yourself: "[*Your name*], *what do you take home from today's session (because you feel it's going to be helpful)?*" And just listen to whatever arises with curiosity.

So, as we are sitting here, say, in a friendly and committed way:

I am coming here today and over the next weeks in order to:

- Work on ways to be helpful to myself.
- Support others as best I can on their journey.
- Be open to the helpfulness of others.

Okay, now start letting that motivation go. Start coming back slowly into the room, noticing your bodies in the chair, feet on the ground, and when you are ready, you can open your eyes.

Module 11: Forgiveness

Aims

- Introduce group to the flow of compassion for others.
- Explore forgiveness.
- Discuss ways to deepen empathy.
- Explore compassion for others in difficult situations.

DOI: 10.4324/9781003202493-12

what is compassion ?
tricky brain

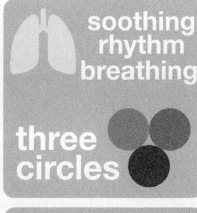
soothing rhythm breathing
three circles

focused attention
mindfulness

feeling safe

other selves
compassionate-self

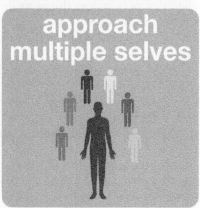
approach multiple selves

encounter the critical-self
and fears

healing from shame
it's not your fault

compassionate letter writing

compassionate assertiveness

compassion for others
forgiveness

Introduction

In this module, we're going to focus on compassion for others. We will focus on forgiveness as an important aspect of compassion for others.

What is forgiveness? It is an adaptive response for dealing with vengeful feelings and desires. A typical reaction when we are hurt is vengeance. Forgiveness gives you the ability to identify your desire to lash out, and not. Rather than act on your desire for vengeance or internalize the hurt, you can activate your compassionate-self and respond with compassion. Forgiveness is more likely if we have effective assertiveness and conflict resolution skills. Importantly, forgiveness is not about condoning being hurt, but in the context of a close relationship, forgiveness is part of repairing the ruptures that damage relationships. So the nature of the relationship is crucial to understanding forgiveness. It is important to understand that forgiveness is not a submissive act. To understand what forgiveness is and is not, please read through Handout 11.2.

Compassion for others is difficult when that conflict is with someone very different from ourselves and/or when that person does things we do not agree with. In moments like these, it is often helpful to think back to some of the basics of CFT and see how they apply to others as well as ourselves. For a moment, try to apply the following statements to others who you are experiencing conflict with.

- All humans are born with a tricky brain.
- We all suffer.
- All humans are born with genes we did not choose and then were socially constructed in an environment we did not choose.
- This is not our fault, but it is our responsibility.

In exploring compassion for others, two important terms to define and differentiate are empathy and sympathy. **Empathy** can be defined as, "the capacity to recognize feelings and understand what is happening within another person and why that might be so without judging them." The more we can understand the emotions of another, the easier it is for us to know how to interact with them. Self-empathy is understanding that we have multiple parts of ourselves and understanding what we think and what we feel. **Sympathy** is simply our emotional reaction(s) to another person's distress—it may be the same or different from the feelings of the other person. With empathy, we tune in to the other person's feelings—knowing those feelings originate in them and not in us. Empathy is important for forgiveness.

Let's try to experience compassion for others with an exercise. While this exercise is typically done in pairs, it has been modified for you to be able to do on your own. For this exercise, we're going to take a minute to practice perspective taking. That is, trying to understand the feelings, thoughts, needs, and intentions of others. As you go through this exercise, you may find it helpful to fill out Handout 11.1. To begin, think of an argument that you had with a person you care about. Try to recognize the potential feelings, thoughts, needs, and intentions of that other person. What might the feelings, thoughts, needs, and intentions of the other person have been? When we better understand the perspective of others, we can more easily feel compassion for them.

Holding good intentions for others can be helpful. For example, think of the difference you might feel in your life if you were to walk around the streets looking at people around you and having compassionate wishes for them to be able to face whatever they need to face in their lives, or compassionate wishes for them to flourish and be happy. Holding these types of wishes and intentions for others is healthy for our brains and our bodies.

Now let's remember when compassion for others tends to be more difficult. It is usually difficult when we are disappointed in somebody or when somebody that we care about lets us down.

Remind yourselves that compassion becomes difficult because our threat system kicks in. When this happens, we can remember to mindfully notice feelings as they arise, slow down our breath, and remember to switch to compassionate-self and compassionate motivation. Remember that forgiveness and compassion for others is good for *you*. To end, please go through the meditation provided at the end of this module.

Compassion for Others in Difficult Situations

Compassion for others in situations of conflict requires:
* **empathy**
* **perspective taking**
* **compassionate motivation**

Describe a situation in which you were in conflict with another as non-judgmentally as possible.

Then, activate your compassionate-self and respond from that position to the following questions:

What might the other person have felt?

What might the other person have thought?

What might the needs of the other person have been?

What intentions might the other person have had?

What are your compassionate wishes for the other person?

Forgiveness

The most essential part of forgiveness is letting go of the angry desire for retaliation and vengeance. This is partly because holding onto these intentions is not good for our body or our brains.

There are different levels of forgiveness. The more we are able to recognize that we are all caught up (with this rather tricky brain) and humans do all kinds of things because of that, the more likely we can move forward. The following are some ideas on what forgiveness is and is not:

IS:

• How we deal with vengeful feelings and desires.

• Part of developing closeness in a relationship.

• More likely to happen if we have good assertiveness and conflict resolution skills.

• Something that we do for ourselves—not for others.

IS NOT:

• Condoning the behavior of somebody else.

• Reconciling with the other person (it could be safer to maintain distance or the other person might not be alive anymore).

• Forgetting.

• Automatically liking the person or needing to be friends with them.

• A way to stop hurting.

• Forgiveness for people does not mean you have to be friends with that person.

Module 11 Review

Core Content Themes

- Compassion for others
    - Others' suffering impacts us
    - When compassion for others is more difficult

- Understanding forgiveness
    - Definition of forgiveness
    - What forgiveness is not
    - Forgiveness is good for YOU

Practice Activities

- Cultivating compassion

Cultivating Compassion

(Note: A digital copy will be provided by your group leader.)

Now that we have developed some practices related to giving compassion to others, let's take a moment to bring our session to a close.

Let's start by consciously re-visiting our intention to develop our compassionate mind and pattern. We start by closing our eyes or looking down and feeling how we are sitting in our chair right now. (Pause 15 seconds.)

Settle into your compassion posture, with your back straight and shoulders in line with your hips, while opening your diaphragm. Now slow your breathing, and with each slower and deeper breath say, slowly and with a friendly tone, "mind slowing down" and then, "body slowing down." Alternate these phrases on each out breath—gradually getting that sense of grounding with a sense of stilling or slowing but also with an alert mind. Notice yourself becoming more grounded. (Pause for a minute or so.)

Now, start tuning in to your inner compassionate mind and pattern. We bring to mind, attend to, and remember the wisdom that you have been developing in our group so far: We all just find ourselves here with a very tricky brain and certain life experiences that have shaped how our minds and bodies work—shaping the version of ourselves that we are. But we have a mind that can learn how to change and make choices, so we are developing the strength and commitment to help ourselves and others address and deal with life and inner difficulties.

Briefly acknowledge yourself for simply being here; with all your doubts, all your resistances, and all your difficulties, but also with the courage and the willingness to go on and to do this path of learning; whatever your current situation is. Acknowledge yourself for giving yourself the opportunity to experience this new learning, for having the courage to stretch your boundaries, even if it's difficult, tricky, and maybe scary. It's scary for everyone.

Acknowledge yourself for being here exactly as you are. Do this in the form of a wish, something like: May I accept myself in this moment of learning exactly as I am; may I give myself all the support and all the kindness I need in this moment; may I accept with compassion all my difficulties, all my doubts; and may I give myself all the compassion I need in this moment.

Gently ask yourself: "[*Your name*], *what do you take home from today's session?*" And just listen to whatever arises with curiosity.

So, as we are sitting here, we also say in a friendly and committed way:

I am coming here today to:

- Work on ways to be helpful to myself.
- Support others as best I can on their journey.
- Be open to the helpfulness of others.

Okay, now start letting that motivation go. We start coming back slowly into the room, noticing our bodies in the chair, feet on the ground, and when you are ready, you can open your eyes.

Module 12: Envisioning a Compassionate Future

Aims

- Review prevention and emergency strategies.
- Envision what a compassionate future involves.
- Engage in gratitude exercise and reflect on group experience.

DOI: 10.4324/9781003202493-13

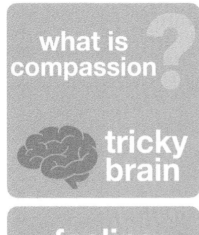

what is compassion ?

tricky brain

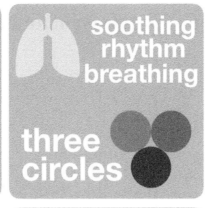

soothing rhythm breathing

three circles

focused attention

mindfulness

feeling safe

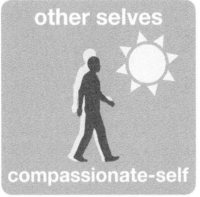

other selves

compassionate-self

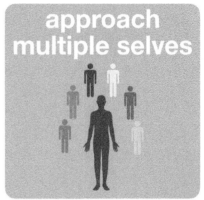

approach multiple selves

encounter the critical-self

and fears

healing from shame

it's not your fault

compassionate letter writing

compassionate assertiveness

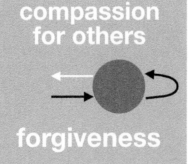

compassion for others

forgiveness

moving forward

with a compassionate mind

Introduction

In this final module, we will explore creating prevention strategies and emergency strategies. Some people might believe that they are only deserving of help or care when things are at their worst. Therefore, developing preventative strategies might be seen as unnecessary or even weak. Let's remember the definition of compassion, which includes not only alleviating suffering when it occurs but also **preventing** suffering when we can. Repeat the mantra, *may I be helpful rather than harmful.*

To begin, let's take a look at Handout 12.1. The purpose of this exercise is to reflect on the different exercises, strategies, and practices that you have been learning over the past several weeks, and see if you can turn them into potential prevention strategies. As we work through this worksheet, try to be mindful of which areas are easier and which are more challenging for you. For example, is it easier or harder to come up with ideas about how to incorporate compassion for self, for others, or receiving compassion?

We thank you for the time and effort that you have put into this group. Take a moment and acknowledge the efforts you have made as well. From your compassionate-self, write a letter to yourself expressing gratitude for your efforts. This may take the form of a compassionate-self from the future, or it may be the compassionate-self that is here right now. For example, you may start by saying:

- "Dear [your name], you are at the end of this path, for now. I want to thank you because…
- You showed the quality of … and this is precious and helpful because…
- During this group, your (fill in behavior) which was helpful because…

Now let's reflect on what we have experienced together as a group. While this would normally be discussed in pairs, you may find it helpful to think about on your own. Ask yourself:

- What were your expectations and what did you learn?
- What did you find difficult in the training?
- What can help you to continue to practice?
- Is there a symbol or an object that expresses what has been valuable for you?

Then to end, a final meditation, "Envisioning a Compassionate Future," is provided at the end of this module. We again thank you for your participation in this group and wish you the best of luck in your future endeavors.

Prevention and Emergency Strategies

Your compassionate-self knows that your tricky brain will lead you in different directions. In fact, we are not expected to stay on track constantly as our tricky brains will likely get in the way. It is very likely that there will be times that we do not remember how to engage in our compassionate-self. Writing some ideas down can bring us back to our compassionate-self and serve as an "emergency backup plan" to help us feel ready to challenge such resistances.

> **Start by slowing your breathing and activating your compassionate-self. As you are engaged in your compassionate-self, respond to the following prompts.**

Which are the situations in which I might need self-compassion the most?	What are compassionate behaviors for that situation?
• _____	• _____
• _____	• _____
• _____	• _____
• _____	• _____
• _____	• _____
Which are the situations in which I might need compassion for others the most?	**What are compassionate behaviors for that situation?**
• _____	• _____
• _____	• _____
• _____	• _____
• _____	• _____
• _____	• _____
Which are the situations in which I might need to be able to accept compassion from others the most?	**What are compassionate behaviors for that situation?**
• _____	• _____
• _____	• _____
• _____	• _____
• _____	• _____
• _____	• _____

Module 12 Review

Core Content Themes

- Prevention strategies and emergency strategies
  - Strategies to feel each of the flows of compassion

- Reflection of group experience

Practice Activities

- Envisioning a compassionate future

Envisioning a Compassionate Future

(Note: A digital copy will be provided by your group leader.)

So for this exercise, first get comfortable in your chairs and adopt your compassionate body posture. Remember to respect the process and prepare your body. Engage your breath as you settle into a soothing rhythm of breathing. Begin to close your eyes if you haven't already done so.

And now imagine that, from now on, you are able to be really compassionate. Imagine, from now on, that being compassionate has become your deepest intention. This future you are imagining will involve a lot of ups and downs, but always with the knowledge that you are continuing to move in a compassionate direction.

And, with your eyes closed, imagine yourself in five years. Really allow yourself to see yourself. Imagine how you appear, knowing that you have been strong and wise. Take note of how the fragility and bravery of being human brings with it a lot of inner authority and natural, authentic kindness. Consider these questions:

- How will you appear? Where are you? (Pause)
- What kind of dreams or goals have you accomplished? (Pause) Now, picture the changes you see in 15 years. (Pause)
- Picture yourself as your compassionate-self at its very best. (Pause)

Now, start to let that visualization go. Connect again with your body in the chair. And when ready, come back into the room.

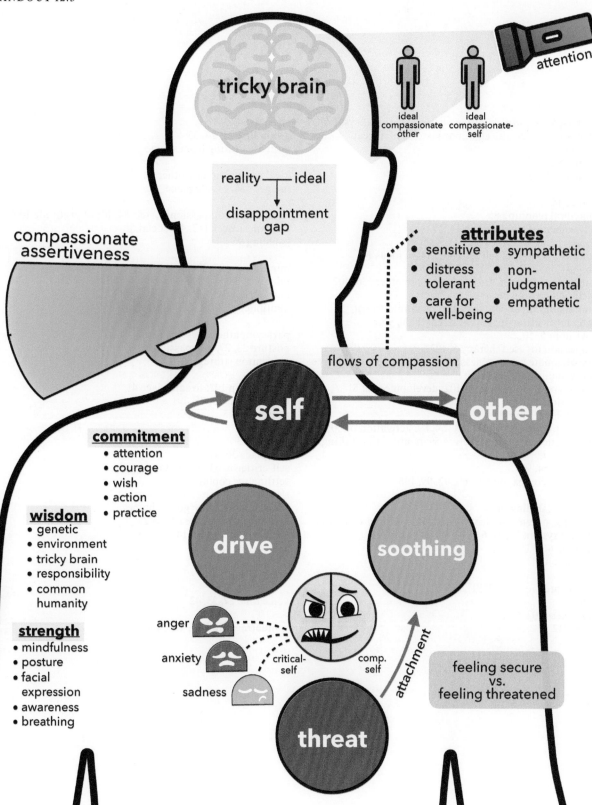

Index

For Product Safety Concerns and Information please contact our EU
representative GPSR@taylorandfrancis.com Taylor & Francis Verlag GmbH,
Kaufingerstraße 24, 80331 München, Germany

Printed and bound by CPI Group (UK) Ltd, Croydon, CR0 4YY

08/06/2025

01897012-0001